ORGANISATIONAL BEHAVIOUR FOR SOCIAL WORK

Gavin Bissell

First published in Great Britain in 2012 by

The Policy Press
University of Bristol
Fourth Floor
Beacon House
Queen's Road
Bristol BS8 1QU
UK
Tel +44 (0)117 331 4054
Fax +44 (0)117 331 4093
e-mail tpp-info@bristol.ac.uk
www.policypress.co.uk

North American office:

The Policy Press
c/o The University of Chicago Press
1427 East 60th Street
Chicago, IL 60637, USA
t: +1 773 702 7700
f: +1 773-702-9756
e:sales@press.uchicago.edu
www.press.uchicago.edu

Cover images reproduced on pages 20 and 92 (c) Canongate Books Ltd

British Library Cataloguing in Publication Data
A catalogue record for this book is available from the British Library.

Library of Congress Cataloging-in-Publication Data
A catalog record for this book has been requested.

ISBN 978 1 84742 279 8 paperback
ISBN 978 1 84742 280 4 hardcover

The right of Gavin Bissell to be identified as author of this work has been asserted by him in accordance with the 1988 Copyright, Designs and Patents Act.

The statements and opinions contained within this publication are solely those of the author and not of The University of Bristol or The Policy Press. The University of Bristol and The Policy Press disclaim responsibility for any injury to persons or property resulting from any material published in this publication.

The Policy Press works to counter discrimination on grounds of gender, race, disability, age and sexuality.

Cover design by The Policy Press
Front cover: image kindly supplied by www.bigstockphoto.com
Printed and bound in Great Britain by Hobbs, Southampton
The Policy Press uses environmentally responsible print partners.

FSC
www.fsc.org
MIX
Paper from
responsible sources
FSC® C020438

Dedicated to the Richmond Road Irregulars
and to temporary social work staff everywhere

Contents

Acknowledgements

Successive year groups of social work students have helped shape the content of this book, typically by contributing examples from their practice placements, both within class dialogue and in their assessed essays at the end of the module. Their module evaluations helped shape the content too, resulting in a final work that captures something of the plain-speaking of the interactive lectures in which we participated over many years. Thanks are due to them all.

Also, I would probably have been sidetracked by research involvement altogether, had it not been for the never-failing interest and support provided by the publishers. Finally, I am grateful to the social work colleagues both academic and practising who commented upon and discussed ideas with me, and especially to Professor Brid Featherstone whose problem-solving approach seldom, if ever, failed, to Dr Kate Karban who read an early draft and made invaluable suggestions, and to Pat Wilkinson (my Head of Department) who moved work around to make writing the book possible. I am also indebted to Dr Paul Sullivan for assistance with Chapter Seven. Any errors in the work are of course mine alone.

Gavin Bissell
Spring 2012

List of figures and tables

Figures

Tables

Introduction

Why do we need a book on organisational behaviour for social work?

In a post-war introductory book on social work for new students, Timms (1970) criticised what he referred to as:

> [the] familiar and misleading story of developments from the time of Christ ('the first social worker') down to the present century, with brief stops in the sixteenth century and a longer pause in the nineteenth. (Timms, 1970, p 1)

The remark demonstrates the down-to-earth, reconstructionist mood of 1960s' social work in Britain, but most interestingly, from the point of view of this book, the 'genuine' account of social work that Timms proceeded to offer began with a chapter entitled 'Social work in organisations'. In this chapter, he called for attention to the fit (or lack of fit) between the social worker, agency and client, yet the chapter did not fully realise Timms' project, perhaps because it went well beyond the space available, in scope. It is therefore in furtherance of that very practical project, of mapping the social work organisation, that this book is undertaken.

Successive government bodies regulating social work training over the past two decades have specifically referred to skills in working in organisations as an area of training and assessment. More recently, job descriptions for social workers increasingly invoke a care management approach, which involves the management, direction and disposal of care resources, including support systems, and this also calls for organisational behaviour knowledge, not least because of the inter-organisational nature of such work.

There is every reason to expect that social work training will maintain its practice focus over the next few years, as the profession continues to follow American models of training imbued with the philosophy of pragmatism. The pressure for practice-linked organisational behaviour texts can therefore be expected to grow. Although there are some very good introductory organisational behaviour textbooks (for example, Handy, 1993; Vecchio, 2000; Buchanan and Huczynski, 2004), these lack attention to the specific gender and care-work aspects that are characteristic of social welfare organisations. Also, organisational behaviour textbooks have been aimed particularly at managers or students of management (indeed, there is a small but growing collection of titles aimed at managers of social services, such as Hafford-Letchfield, 2008, and Hughes and Wearing, 2007).

This book seeks to locate these two types of publication within the larger field of social work organisational behaviour, clarifying the connections between them, while providing a critical commentary upon organisational behaviour textbooks from the standpoint of social services and their users and workers. In taking a 'bottom–up' approach to social work organisations, rather than a management approach, it draws on the tradition of American textbooks such as Gibelman and Furman (2008), taking into account the specific UK legal and policy context.

In aiming to meet the growing demand for an organisational behaviour textbook focusing upon the specific experience of welfare organisations, this book is not intended to break new theoretical ground in organisational behaviour, or to add any new dimension to social work practice, but rather to tie in experience and learning to organisational behaviour themes. The realism of some traditional organisational behaviour concepts, such as 'grapevines' and 'watch your back cultures', can help make sense of welfare settings, as well as being a useful bridge between the completion of social work training and the take-up of post-qualifying employment.

The book's aims are therefore to invite the reader to reflect on the way in which social work and social care are organised and, especially, to explore the operation of power and inequality within organisations, at the individual, group and inter-organisational levels, while examining the implications of all of the above for individual personal and professional development.

Why should students and social workers study organisational behaviour?

There is a significant overlap between the central task and skill requirements of social work, on one hand, and the know–how of organisational working, on the other (Hafford-Letchfield, 2008). This is because all social work takes place in an organisational context. For example, research has shown that social work decision-making is affected by organisational context (O'Sullivan, 1999); that the social worker's attitude to service users is affected by organisational culture (Hawkins and Shohet, 2006); and that good assessment and risk management depend upon effective communication in the organisation (Williams, 2006). As noted above, Timms (1970) maintained that the organisational context of social work affected not only the practice of the social worker, but also the behaviour of the client. He identified, for example, the differences between social work in a medical setting and social work in a juvenile justice setting, both for the social worker and for the service user.

Timms also argued, incidentally, that because of this 'organisational factor' the existence and teaching of *generic* social work skills might itself be considered problematic. For example, a service user's loss within the organisational context of social work with older people is not quite the same as loss with a family whose child has been released for adoption within the organisational context of children's services. That is, although from a psychodynamic point of view the loss process may be similar, the different organisational settings construct the social dimension of the loss quite differently.

As Timms was writing on the eve of the Local Authority (Social Services) Act 1970, which gave rise to expanded provision of personal social services by local authorities, it is a moot point whether or not he would have argued against the generic training that followed it. In an authoritative earlier report on social work training, Younghusband (1947) had identified major differences between the various organisational settings of social work, but did not conclude that this rendered generic training impossible.

Either way, organisational setting is acknowledged to exert a significant influence upon social work practice, and therefore on social work training, regardless of whether it is specialist or generic. Precisely how this happens will be examined in this book.

Reading this book should help those interested in the operation of welfare: to critically review the knowledge and understanding of theoretical frameworks relating to organisations; to understand the contribution of different approaches to management, leadership and quality in public and independent services; to locate professionalism in a bureaucratic context; and to contextualise personal development. In particular, the book should help the reader to critically evaluate recent concepts from a range of sources relating to social work organisation and management, and to apply this understanding to practice situations.

Management studies or organisational behaviour?

The study of organisational behaviour was regarded until relatively recently as the domain of the budding manager. From the 1980s, new managers in social services departments were expected to 'skill up' to the level of trained managers in local authorities (see Andrew, 1999). Coulshed et al (2006) argue that, by the end of the 1980s, it was increasingly necessary to the delivery of good services for social workers to understand how organisational systems work. Many of the reasons Coulshed et al (2006) gave for studying the 'management point of view' hold true for studying organisational behaviour: self-defence; avoiding scapegoating; understanding when the organisation rather than the individual is at fault and adopting a critical attitude towards standards.

Social workers now work to managerialist agendas (Balloch et al, 1999), and many of the organisational behaviour skills deployed by managers are (or are similar to) established social work skills, suggesting significant day-to-day use of managerial concepts by social workers. Furthermore, the growth of the care management paradigm in social work, from the 1990s through to the present day, has made the study of organisational behaviour increasingly necessary to social workers, not least because the language of care management is extensively permeated by organisational behaviour concepts.

So, why should the social worker study organisational behaviour, rather than management studies, on which there are many good textbooks in existence? Although the view from the manager's office is both interesting and useful (Glastonbury et al, 1987; Coulshed et al, 2006), it is in fact organisational behaviour

---

3

generally, not just a specific focus on the manager's perspective, that is of interest to *every* employee in a social welfare organisation. Non-managers do not, typically, identify themselves with this subject but knowledge of organisational behaviour is relevant to their work. Finally, an additional reason for studying organisational behaviour, and one rarely discussed in the literatures of either social work or organisational behaviour, is that social work and the study of organisational behaviour have an interesting shared history, stretching back to the late 19th century. This will be examined in **Chapter Eleven** on organisational change.

Who might read this book

There is a raft of post-qualifying (PQ) training in social work at present, as employers seek to implement a salary scale progression that is linked to professional development; there is also the new Approved Mental Health Professional training. These initiatives seem to call for some input around professional practice in organisations too.

Anyone interested in social work, social care or welfare may find this a relevant subject to study, including users of services provided by organisations in this sector. Indeed, it is often those on the receiving end of an organisation's services who experience organisational dynamics most acutely.

Themes of the book

Diversity is at the forefront of current social work theory and must be considered as a salient theme when examining organisational behaviour concepts. Within diversity, gender issues specific to social work organisations, such as fragmentary career structure, team working, communication and management styles, form a key theme of this book. A critical reception of organisational behaviour concepts, ideas and language must therefore form one of the salient themes of any reading straddling the two areas, and previous writing on gender and organisations has been useful here (Kanter, 1977; Savage and Witz, 1992; Roper, 1994; Wilson, 1995).

The theoretical problems faced by the field of organisational behaviour seem to recur from generation to generation. Possible explanations for this are complex and beyond the scope of this book. However, the diversity issues identified in successive chapters reflect something of the cyclical, unresolved character of central organisational behaviour problems, and are well worth further study on this account alone.

Last but not least, as noted earlier, the service user is an integral part of the social work organisation and therefore also forms an important theme throughout the book.

Plan of the book

The treatment of organisational behaviour in this book is succinct and practical, largely avoiding abstract debates such as that concerning the difference between a group and a team, or that concerning the ontological status of organisations. It briefly states each of the main organisational behaviour themes and theories in turn, before drawing in social work literature and examples to flesh them out in an applied way.

The enduring format of organisational behaviour textbooks approaches the various aspects of organisational behaviour as relatively autonomous subjects, each with its own chapter. Although organisational structures and cultures could also provide a useful framework, the traditional approach has been adhered to in this book:

- **Chapter One** provides an overview of theories of the organisation, providing an overview of the organisational behaviour literature;
- **Chapter Two** deals with motivation in social work organisations, looking specifically at the impact of the organisation upon the motivation of the individual social worker, including staff retention and career progression;
- **Chapter Three** looks at communication in social work organisations (a favourite topic of government inquiries into child protection tragedies);
- **Chapter Four** examines the impact of the organisation on social work decision-making, risk and error – important issues in social work practice;
- **Chapter Five** investigates team roles in social work, with some consideration of theories of primary groups and area teams;
- **Chapter Six** considers the impact of organisational culture upon the practice of social work, and especially upon diversity;
- **Chapter Seven** assesses the value of organisational models of learning;
- **Chapter Eight** applies organisational behaviour theories of leadership and management to social work, especially the theory of distributed management;
- **Chapter Nine** looks at specific management strategies in social work: (management by objectives and total quality management);
- **Chapter Ten** considers power in organisations, with particular reference to an important issue for social work – service user power and empowerment;
- **Chapter Eleven** looks at organisational change in social workers' organisations, with particular attention to reorganisation of social services and convergence with the voluntary sector; and
- **Chapter Twelve** provides a conclusion to the book, looking at policy and practice changes in social work organisations.

CHAPTER ONE

Organisational theories and contexts

What you will learn in this chapter
- The origins of organisational theory
- Different types of organisational structure
- How organisational context can influence the practice of social work
- Effects of organisational context upon social work practice
- The relevance of scientific management approaches
- The connections between bureaucracy and control

Introduction

The aim of this chapter is to provide a brief overview of the study of the structure of the workplace, from its origins around the beginning of the 20th century to the most recent manifestations of scientific management. How effective has the scientific approach to organisation structure been in improving efficiency? How appropriate is it for understanding welfare organisations? To what extent does the bureaucracy of social welfare organisations result in a loss of job control by the social worker?

Origins of organisational behaviour

A major recent textbook of organisational behaviour defined an organisation as:

> A social arrangement for achieving controlled performance in pursuit of collective goals. (Buchanan and Huczynski, 2004, p 6)

Using this definition, the group, or even the family, is an organisation to the extent that it has collective goals and arrangements for achieving controlled performance in pursuit of them. Indeed, the definition implies that there are *no* individuals isolated absolutely from organisations. Given this claim to the ubiquity of organisational forms, it may seem strange that organisational behaviour has been so neglected in social work.

This may in part be because of the way in which debate about early bureaucracies developed in England. Macpherson (1973) argued that, since the philosophers Thomas Hobbes and John Locke, English political theory has taken place within a debate about the relationship between the state and the individual, and a good deal of political and social theory has been informed by this binary opposition (theories of class structure notwithstanding).

During the 1920s, at the time when the industrial welfare arm of English social work was investigating obstacles to the efficiency of the workforce and of individual workers in particular, the mental health arm of social work was developing its interest in Freud (Younghusband, 1947). The post-war focus on Freudian Attachment Theory, for example in the journal *Family Casework,* illustrates the tendency of social workers to think in individualising terms quite late into the 20th century. A focus upon individual problems tends to decentre contextual analysis of any kind and, despite efforts to embed class analysis into social work training from the beginning of the 20th century (Webb, 1926), individualising tendencies persisted. The analysis of organisations has therefore fallen between the relatively high-level sociological concepts of state and class, on one hand, and those of family, group and individual behaviour, on the other.

Perhaps because of this individualising focus in the UK, organisational theory has mainly been 'imported' from elsewhere. There were pioneers in Britain, Europe and elsewhere during the 19th century, including work by Herbert Spencer, where the co-existence of the virtual anarchism of *The man versus the state* (1884) and the study of organisational development in his book *Principles of sociology* (1874–85) would be worthy of a book in itself. However, much of the organisational theory in use today is American in origin, with the works of Max Weber, Karl Marx and others refracted through the prism of American organisational behaviour literature (Coulshed et al, 2006). Although there are a number of classic texts of organisational behaviour (such as Simey, 1937; Simon, 1945; Barnard, 1948; Simon et al, 1950), the critical perspectives that have come to the fore in the literature of organisational behaviour in recent years are also valuable and necessary adjuncts to its study, if an unthinking bias is to be avoided (see for example Jackson and Carter, 2000).

Organisational structures

A useful place to start in understanding theories of organisation is to begin by distinguishing organisational *structures*, for example the organisation of the workplace or the disposition of departments within the organisation, from organisational *processes*, which include behaviours within the organisation (see Buchanan and Huczynski, 2004, ch 4). Jackson and Carter (2000) claim that it is the processes that constitute the organisation, since without people it does not exist, which leads us to speculate upon what exactly constitutes a social services organisation. Is it the offices, the service users, the service unit sites or the employees?

The study of the 'where' of offices or service units has been relatively neglected in social work (Godkin, 1980; Wilkinson and Bissell, 2005), while there has been a tendency to focus upon social work relationships in a relatively disembodied way (Wilkinson and Bissell, 2007; Galloway et al, 2008). It will be important to avoid a similar bias in studying social work organisations.

The core structure of the organisation

Figure 1.1: The five basic parts of organisations

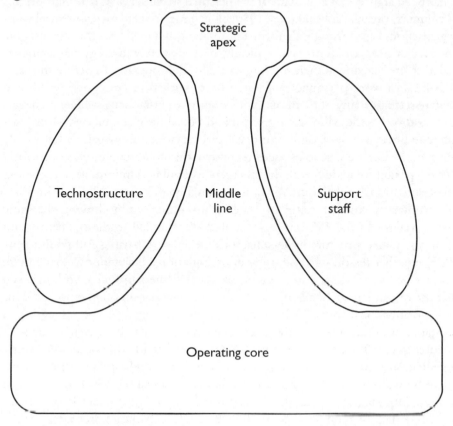

Strategic
apex

Technostructure

Middle
line

Support
staff

Operating core

Source: Abridged from Mintzberg, 1979, p 20.

Why doesn't the social worker's organisational structure look like Mintzberg's (1979) diagram (in Figure 1.1)? There are several reasons why it does not. First, if the setting is a local authority, the roughly 30% of the organisation that is taken up with support functions (for example the legal department, the estates division, human resources) and technostructure (for example, the policy and planning department) is usually sited elsewhere and not often likely to be in the social worker's path. Second, the 'operating core' in social services is a very broad base, made up of area teams and service units in diverse service divisions, and the visible parts of the organisation tend to be 'horizontal' in organisational terms. As will be seen, these visible parts of the organisation also tend to be the chief frame of reference for social workers. Third, as Lipsky (1980) argued, for most purposes the team or service unit setting in which the individual works *is* the organisation, or rather it appears to be to the individual.

Organisational convergence between the statutory and voluntary sectors

It has been argued that almost all of the personal social services had their origins in voluntary organisations (Harvey, 1980), which means that few, if any, social work organisations have sprung fully formed into being as a public sector organisation. Social work organisations will typically have grown with regional branches added as they expanded their funding base and their operations. Before the early 1970s, social work personnel will often have worked in combined health and welfare settings, many of them under the control of non-social welfare managers such as those in the Ministry of Health and Social Services. Harvey (1980) has suggested that voluntary and statutory social services only began to be sharply distinguished in the period of social reconstruction following the Second World War – a period coinciding with the emergence of public administration textbooks of organisational behaviour. Yet it was arguably the increasing specification of voluntary sector provision by state sector purchasers following the 'new managerialism' of the 1980s (Clarke et al, 2000) that led to the standardisation of organisational structure in personal social services (Charities Aid Foundation, 1993) (another reason why the study of organisational behaviour in social work has received increased attention in recent years). Others in social work believed that the organisational 'shake up' of the new managerialism offered potential for new organisational forms in line with an ethos of caring, empowerment and resistance against oppression (Mullender and Perrott, 1997), as well as using an essential skill in the repertoire of professional social work, that of implementing organisational change. The convergence (or persistent similarity) of organisational forms between voluntary sector and public sector social services is perhaps due to the continuing (and increasing) need to maintain tight financial controls on front-line staff. As Robbins (1993) observes, the 'mechanical bureaucracy' is the organisational structure that best supports this tight control strategy (see the mechanistic structure in Figure 1.2).

The kind of flexible, organic structure (see Figure 1.2) required for a strategy of maximising innovative responsiveness to customers (Senge, 1990) must somehow be mapped onto this. Robbins (1993) argues that, in the private sector, a hybrid structure of tight hierarchy, supplemented by fluid, flat, self-managing teams at the periphery, is characteristic for example of firms producing short production runs of 'copycat' goods. While there is no intrinsic necessity for social service organisations to mirror the structure of organisations in the private sector, it is possible to see a similar formation, reformation and dissolution of teams and service units to meet changing conceptions of service user need in the public sector, particularly in adult services.

Reflective point:Think about how the two structures in Figure 1.2 reflect your experiences in the workplace?

Figure 1.2: Mechanistic versus organic structures

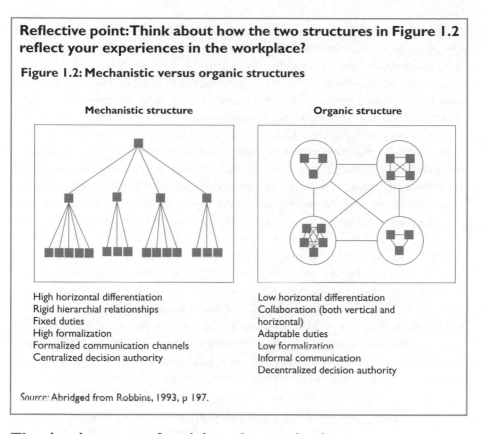

Mechanistic structure	Organic structure

High horizontal differentiation
Rigid hierarchial relationships
Fixed duties
High formalization
Formalized communication channels
Centralized decision authority

Low horizontal differentiation
Collaboration (both vertical and horizontal)
Adaptable duties
Low formalization
Informal communication
Decentralized decision authority

Source: Abridged from Robbins, 1993, p 197.

The development of social work organisations

In their innovative work, Coulshed et al (2006) argued that a grounding in management ideas was a useful preparation for social work practitioners as well as managers, and they offered a Cook's tour of some landmark thinkers in management considered to be of relevance to social work. Coulshed et al's (2006) refer to Henri Fayol (1949) as the pioneer management theorist, but the papers of the Charity Organisation Society (COS) in the 1890s show that early social work methods displayed a strong organisational and administrative awareness of their own before Fayol's first publication on the administration of organisations. Indeed, Octavia Hill and C.S. Loch, two luminaries of the COS, were arguably of their time in opposing the autocratic practices of some London charities with their scientific, bureau–rational approaches, much as the career managers of companies formed following the Joint Stock and Limited Liability Acts promoted their scientific management approach (Loch, 1905).

The dialogue between social work and business is a longstanding one; their influence has been, and continues to be, reciprocal. In 1916 an Act of Parliament gave the government powers to induce factories employing young people on night war work, or work with dangerous substances, to engage a social worker (or 'welfare supervisor') to safeguard the personal lives of these young people, who were perceived to be vulnerable in the sometimes dirty and unsanitary conditions that had previously been largely the preserve of men. The welfare workers built upon the already existing practices of the 'social secretaries' employed by the larger firms from the end of the nineteenth century. For example, Agatha Harrison, the first university welfare work lecturer, started her career as a welfare secretary with Boot's Chemists in Nottingham, and subsequently worked as a welfare administrator with Metal Box in Hull (Harrison, 1956). These workers, trained on university courses such as that offered by the London School of Economics from 1905 onwards, concerned themselves with the general health, well-being and problems of the employees. With the worsening economic conditions in the early 1930s, there was an attempt to change their collective image to that of 'labour managers' and this in turn fed the new discipline of personnel management (see *The Welfare Worker*, 1920–31; *Labour Management and Personnel Administration*, 1931–46).

The social worker as industrial welfare worker was clearly bound by the aims of the organisation in which she worked. She spent much of her time doing sickness visiting and attending to obstacles in the lives of employees that inhibited their efficiency, for example, cleanliness and bad language at work were considered welfare issues (Harrison, 1956). This focus of industrial social work on efficiency has a long history (Shadwell, 1909), although Mintzberg (1983) noted that efficiency cannot, of itself, constitute a valid organisational goal or mission (Drucker [1955] appears to have held a similar view).

How does organisational context influence social work practice?

The early history of social work illustrates how the organisational context of social work has an important effect upon the relationship between the social worker and her client. The influence of a very different type of organisational context will now be explored in the following case study.

ARMY SOCIAL WORK

Social work recruiting poster, January 1960

Social work in the US Army

Wiest and Devis (1971) have argued that, as a host organisation, the US Army has provided a particularly conducive setting to social work during the twentieth century. While the professions of Army psychologist and psychiatrist remained static in numbers between 1942 and the 1970s, social workers grew to exceed both professional groups in numbers. While the former professions experienced recruitment difficulties, social work flourished. Why was this? How could social work thrive in an admittedly authoritarian organisation, while other, cognate professional groups did not?

The need for all three professional groups was recognised widely during the First World War. Mental illness casualties formed an unacceptably high proportion of all casualties, and represented a significant loss of manpower (see Wilson and Hammerton's 1919 *The Great War* Volume 13 for a contemporary account of this). US Army command looked at the French and British responses to mental illness and were dissatisfied with their own provisions. At that time, the British tended to take men out of the front line into mental hospitals for individual psychotherapeutic treatment (Wilson and Hammerton, 1919), but the rate of return to combat was considered disappointing by the US military. The French approach, combining hospital treatment with disciplinary responses, was also deemed unsatisfactory. By the end of the First World War, however, community psychiatry was an embryonic form of alternative treatment that was to develop during the Second World War and after in Britain and elsewhere. Also, the Red Cross had been asked for social workers, and of these over 700 were to be placed in the US Army by the end of the Second World War.

Why did the US Army prove so conducive to social work? Wiest and Devis (1971) identify a number of possible factors. First, psychiatry had found a relatively straightforward route into the Army by following the route of army medical officers, whose rank and role had been long established. Psychiatric social work, a newly emerging role struggling for professional status, benefited directly from its connection with psychiatry, eventually being recognised as a professional group by the US Army in 1946 and accordingly granted officer status. Second, some of the professional aims of social work coincided with those of Army command, namely, as far as possible to keep people functioning in their normal lives (what came to be known as the 'crisis intervention' model of brief intervention). Third, and perhaps most important of all, social workers had a social model of mental illness that overlapped with the Army's environmental understanding of mental illness in soldiers and of the unique situation of the soldier. The soldier is subjected to family separation, frequent home moves and a sharp dislocation of home and work environments.

The overlap between the organisational aims of the Army and the professional aims of social work, on one hand, and between Army welfare philosophy and social work's knowledge base, on the other, led to the success of Army social work. Wiest and Devis (1971) argue that, in contrast, the medical model of individual treatment in psychiatry showed, under military stimulation, moves towards forms of community psychiatry after the Second World War; and psychology, with its individualising approach, experienced the biggest Army recruitment difficulties of any profession in this area.

It is tempting to expand at this point on the difficulties of practising social work in medical organisations, or within penal organisations. Perhaps we should not leave this discussion of Army social work without recording, as Wiest and Davis (1971) did, that there is a profound difference between the authoritarian structure of the Army and the democratic structure of civil society.

Do organisations control the workplace?

Apart from through their philosophy, ethos and organisational objectives, how do organisations influence the way social workers work with clients? An obvious way is by controlling the physical space of the workplace. Millward et al (2007) studied the use of hot-desking in the finance industry to find out how it affected work. Hot-desking is used increasingly in social work settings, and refers to any arrangement in which individual workers do not have assigned workstations but work at any vacant desk. It seems worth pointing out that social workers' responses to this situation are by no means all negative: some appreciate the opportunity to move around and sit next to different colleagues, and feel that, after a long stint in a shared office, a break at a desk in another room can be a real tonic. Millward et al (2007), however, found that there were other effects besides convenience: those workers assigned a regular desk tended to identify themselves with a particular team (see **Chapter Five**) and there are consequences of team membership for decision making in social work (**Chapter Four**), as we will see later. Conversely, those workers hot-desking tended to identify themselves more with the organisation as a whole and with its objectives, rather than with those of the individual team.

Organisations can also influence the way social workers work with their clients by constructing the teams in which they work. One example of this is hospital-based care management: the working team is likely to consist of social workers, nurses, occupational therapists and community care assistants, often working in the same office space or at adjacent desks. What effect does the constitution of the working team have upon the work of the individual social worker? We might also consider the physical separation of intake and casework teams in this context. (Team composition will be examined later in **Chapter Five**.)

Organisations may also influence the way social workers work through their workplace culture (for example, in a faith-based organisation) (see **Chapter Six**), or through their characteristic patterns of communication (see **Chapter Three**), through the style of leadership (**Chapter Eight**), or through the adoption of a particular management strategy (see **Chapter Nine**).

Scientific management approaches

Analysis of workplace organisation also includes a range of studies dealing with efficiency, such as the scientific management studies of Taylor (1911) and Gilbreth (1911), and some of the methods employed by the motor manufacturer Henry Ford until the Second World War.

Taylor's four principles

Frederick Winslow Taylor researched worker productivity, looking at the best way of performing each work task, the time it required, materials needed and the work sequence. From this work Taylor developed four principles of scientific management:

1. Develop a scientific work methodology based on analysis of the tasks.
2. Select, train and develop all employees.
3. Provide instruction, supervision and performance management.
4. Allocate the work so that managers plan and supervise the work and employees undertake the tasks.

Frederick Winslow Taylor

To what extent can Taylor's (1911) 'four principles' be applied to social work?

In social services, the defined tasks of service provision initially developed in an organic manner, but with the new managerialism of the 1980s came a clearer definition of the roles of managers, as well as more systematic recruitment and selection, the regularised training of new employees (including induction into organisational culture), and regularised supervision. The application of Taylor's principles can therefore be traced to the present day.

Critics of the work study process have argued that it can lead to deskilling, is authoritarian, and that it prescribes tasks and compulsory operational methods, ignoring motivation and accelerating staff turnover.

It is interesting, in passing, to note that Tayloristic work study methods were introduced into the Soviet Union between 1917 and 1929 (Peci, 2009). Peci suggests that this strategy of workplace organisation was tied to the project of modernism in this context, rather than to capitalistic management strategies. This is encouraging for those inclined to view Taylorism as something more than a profit mechanism, but does not rebut the accusation that in application the methods may be authoritarian.

Gilbreth: time and motion

The time and motion study of husband and wife team Frank Bunker Gilbreth and Lillian Moller Gilbreth (Gilbreth, 1911) also survives in the social work workplace in the ergonomic, semicircular desk, which made its appearance in some area social services offices in the 1990s, and perhaps also the breakdown of interpersonal skills into eye contact and eyebrow flash as seen in some social work communication skills texts. A less obvious distant relation of the Gilbreths' work is the breakdown of jobs into their component skill areas, such as the National Occupational Standards and social work Key Roles. Car manufacturer Henry Ford took these scientific approaches further with job disassembly and the development of the production line just before the First World War (Ford, 1922). There is perhaps a distant echo of this in the social work cycle, which bears comparison with trouble-shooting procedures used in the chemical process and other continual process industries in the mid-twentieth century.

Deskilling

Galbraith (1958) maintained that jobs are increasingly intellectually skilled, but Braverman (1974) argued that the worker's knowledge and skill is gradually transferred to the organisation as a result of the drive for efficiency and that this has resulted in *deskilling*. That is to say, a latent function of scientific management approaches has been to separate out the component skills of a work role and assign these as routinised tasks to lower-skilled workers.

Harris (1998, 2000), Jones (2001), and Butler and Drakeford (2005) have described this deskilling in social work. For example, Harris (1998) maintains that social work skills have been transferred to paperwork (such as assessment forms administered by unqualified workers). Dressel (1987) argued that the separation of intake teams from long-term teams has had a similar impact, and that many of these forms of workplace organisation have been applied in social work in order to control emotional labour and women's behaviour, deskilling their roles. Finally, Butler and Drakeford (2005) argue that care management has become the 'handmaid' of the health service and that tick-box assessment has taken the place of skilled roles.

Yet there is a defence of these methods, which may hold true for the training of social workers. Recruits develop very quickly from unskilled to efficient workers, helped by clear rules and procedures; the process is impersonal, fair and non-discriminatory. Buchanan and Huczynski (2004) observe that perhaps Taylorism as a whole does not simply ignore intrinsic interest in the work. Perhaps we are better able to perform dull paperwork tasks if we have in sight wider goals, such as those that social workers often bring to their jobs. However, motivation is a topic worthy of examination in its own right (see **Chapter Two**).

'McDonaldisation'

Ritzer (1993) expanded the deskilling argument with the 'McDonaldisation' thesis. What he meant by this was that consumerism also had an impact upon workplace organisation, insofar as the search for a consistent standard of service in an age of global distribution of brands had lent additional pressure to the disassembly of tasks and the routinisation of their component parts. In the social work literature, it has been argued that care management is the McDonaldisation of social casework

(Dustin, 2007), but how far McDonaldisation impacts on social work is debatable. See Table 1.1 for a comparison of the key aspects of McDonaldisation and ideas about ways that this is reflected in social work practice.

Table 1.1: McDonaldisation in social work

Characteristic of McDonaldisation	Examples from social work
Efficient, high speed service provision	Process stage targets
Good value and minimum waste	Compulsory competitive tendering and service level agreements
Predictable service irrespective of time or location	Telephone protocols
Staff performing a limited range of tasks in a precisely detailed way	Core assessments

Some writers have pointed out weaknesses of the McDonaldisation thesis, namely, that multi-skilled employees are more useful to employers, that the application of information technology creates new skills, and that Ritzer assumes that labour costs are critical, when in fact they are a diminishing fraction of total expenditure (consider the rising proportion of social services expenditure consumed by capital costs such as building modernisation and maintenance). Perhaps most important of all, many workers say they like some forms of service standardisation, and consider services to be improved by it.

While social workers might have some sense of improvements in service delivery, front-line service workers might feel that some control over their jobs has been sacrificed to protocols and standardised services. This view supports a picture of a dual labour market (Robbins, 1993) in social services.

Rational models

However, not everyone agrees with this view of care management, some (eg Lymbery, 1998) see the addition of new skills in the move towards care management, including numerical upskilling and taking over file keeping. Yet this might be less a result of workplace analysis, and more the outcome of what Weber (1964) described as the tendency of organisations toward rational bureaucracy and a rule-following culture. An implication of this 'longer view' is that the move towards 'post-bureaucratic' organisational forms may perhaps be more apparent than real. Postle (2002) takes a similar view of care management, seeing it as yet another step in the rationalisation of social work. Another way of viewing care management is as an inevitable accompaniment of technology-driven, information-rich progress: Galbraith (1958), Senge (1990) and other proponents of the 'Knowledge Society' have argued that a process of upskilling is occurring generally. Lymbery (1998) applies this positive view to care management, a sort of 'we're all managers now' argument.

Bureaucracy and control

Opinions vary on the bureaucratic nature of social work organisations, and on the extent to which this is a 'bad' thing. Schofield (2001) sees the bureaucratic legacy of social work organisations as a bulwark against the perceived political fads and managerial fashions faced by British social services since the 1980s. Similarly, Briscoe (2007) views bureaucracy positively as a shield for the temporal flexibility of professional service workers. Briscoe argues bureaucracy facilitates client information sharing between professionals and standardises client–worker relations, which means that an individual worker's absence does not obstruct the provision of a service. Bureaucracy creates the illusion of continuity of service, despite manifest discontinuities in staffing, personnel, and even service unit sites.

It is possible to see virtually the same organisational features as undermining professional autonomy and causing deskilling (Kitchener, 2000). Scott (1969) argued that American welfare organisations are bureaucracies primarily designed for administering benefits, and this brings them into conflict with the independent professional; in other words, there is an inbuilt tendency for the organisation to be experienced as controlling. Simpson and Simpson (1969) maintained that welfare organisations are more controlling than other organisations because their employees are mostly female. Their argument was that, because society does not perceive women to be as invested in their work as male employees, male senior managers are able to exploit societal bias by making front-line (female) employees more accountable. Whether or not this was true in the 1960s is difficult to know for sure, but the argument is unlikely to receive the same credibility today.

The idea that organisational history in general is best understood as a history of control is discussed by Victor and Stephens (1994) and Jermier and Clegg (1994), but control in organisations is exercised in different ways at different times, from Tayloristic workplace control, job rotation and workgroups (Mayo 1933), to learning culture and mission statements (Senge, 1990).

In a comparatively early piece of research, Smith (1969) identified several ways in which welfare organisations exercise control. First, consider the use of statistical records as bureaucratic control: comparatively recent innovations such as worker performance statistics, as well as service delivery statistics, can be seen to facilitate hierarchical control, in Smith's terms. Opinions vary about the significance of supervision in social work (Hawkins and Shohet, 2000; Gray et al, 2010), but both Etzioni (1969) and Smith (1969) viewed it as a form of control, supporting the contemporary view that the emphasis upon supervision in social work represents an increase in the control of welfare organisations over individuals.

Third, Smith argues that 'the desire to define and isolate categories of persons'(1969, p 88) creates a type of organisational environment restricting professional choice and creating client dependency. Total institutions (Goffman, 1957) are clear examples of this and there are still many of these around in social work, despite the move towards community-based care over the past 30–40 years. However, there is also a sense in which, at a very abstract level, control by the workplace organisation over the employee can be viewed as the 'social glue' which replaced the community and craft associations of an earlier historical period as the link between the individual and society (Tonnies, 1955; Durkheim, 1964), even though some writers (Tonnies in particular) clearly had mixed feelings about this. So, even though control may appear authoritarian, we might then ask what could be concluded if workplace organisations were more loosely connected with the individual.

It has also been argued that the extent to which a welfare organisation is controlling of its social workers depends on the individual manager and upon the social worker. O'Sullivan (1999) maintained that, despite the increased control brought to welfare by new managerialism in the 1990s, a sympathetic line manager, especially one with social work values rather than purely managerial ones, could provide a congenial environment for social work practice, especially if the individual social worker asserts professional values and does not uncritically accept managerial initiatives.

Alvesson and Wilmott (2004) argue that the regulation of organisational identity is also a potential avenue of organisational control. They contend that strategies such as creating team identity are not necessarily a good thing, because they can restrict the range of options in individual decision-making. In their study of nursing staff Pratt and Rafaeli (1997) found that whilst charge nurses wanted ward staff to wear civilian dress in order to move patients into a 'going home' mindset, the auxiliaries wanted to wear scrubs (a kind of operating theatre 'uniform'), because they associated them with comparatively high-status jobs like surgical nursing. Both these studies suggest that organisational control of identity is a contestable area.

▶KEY LEARNING POINTS

- Most organisational theory originates from the United States
- The organisational structure of welfare organisations does not easily map onto the mechanistic or organic structures found in the private sector
- The organisational context can influence social work practice in a number of ways
- Scientific management approaches may provide structured job roles and training, but potentially deskill employees
- Welfare organisations are by their nature simultaneously enabling and controlling

▶SEMINAR ORIENTATION: ARE WELFARE ORGANISATIONS INCREASINGLY EXERCISING CONTROL?

Reading: Buchanan and Huczynski (2004), Chapter 13.

▶EXERCISE: THE HOMICIDE DEPARTMENT

Read David Simon's (2008) *Homicide*, pp 18-23, and answer the following questions:

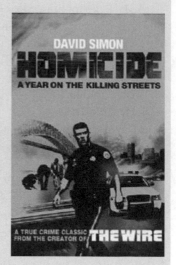

1. What is the structure of the homicide department, and how does it affect (a) the motivation of individual detectives, (b) relations within each of the teams?
2. What is the leadership style of each captain, and what effect does it have upon the work of each team?
3. Compare 'red ball' homicides and child protection deaths. What similarities and differences can you find in the way the organisation responds to each?

CHAPTER TWO

Motivation: what makes social work a good job?

What you will learn in this chapter

- Relationship between motivation and stress in contemporary social work practice
- Job satisfaction and career pathways
- Classic studies of motivational behaviour and relevance to social work
- Motivations particular to social work and care work
- Gendered dimensions of motivation
- Connections between intrinsic and extrinsic motivations

Introduction

This chapter will look at motivation in social work organisations, and at the various factors that impinge upon it. In particular we will look at the relationship between motivation, working conditions and job satisfaction as an issue in current social work practice. The chapter reviews the classical theories of motivation found in the organisational behaviour literature, and critically explores the application of them in social work organisations. There is also an existing specialist literature on the motivation of social workers, and the overall aim of this chapter is to merge organisational behaviour concepts with this specialist literature.

Other important factors, such as doing valuable work, responsibility and personal growth as motivational factors in work, and religious motivations, are discussed, as well as gender issues, in particular, how men feel about work in social work organisations. What motivations do men have to enter a perceived 'female' occupation, and how, if at all, does the motivation of male social workers differ from that of their female counterparts in the same organisations? Finally, we will review theories of intrinsic and extrinsic motivations and their relevance for social work.

Why be a social worker?

Reviewing recent issues of the 'trade press' of social work, the casual reader might be forgiven for thinking that all was far from well with the motivation of social workers. For example, in April 2009, *Community Care* magazine quoted the director of the Association of Directors of Children's Services as saying that he wanted to restore morale to children's social work, stating "Social workers have said to me, 'Why would you want to enter this profession?'" (Bromley-Derry quoted in Lombard, 2009a). It is commonly said of social work that it is a particularly stressful job, with stress arising from, amongst other sources, the daily activity of working with the strong emotions of people in distress and families in crisis. When *Community Care* surveyed its readers in April 2009, responses from 450 social workers led it to report that 72% faced burnout from making difficult decisions under stress (Lombard, 2009b). The periodical adduced this reason, together with those of excessive workloads, poor supervision, the tarnished public image of social work, and a climate of fear of catastrophe, for the low morale of social workers.

Figure 2.1: *Community Care* **reader survey 2009**

Job satisfaction

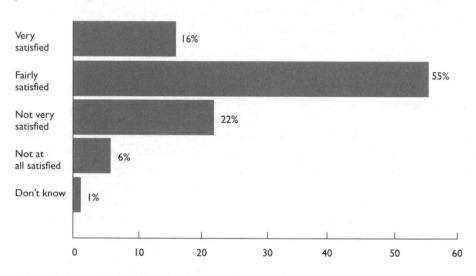

How employers are performing on working conditions

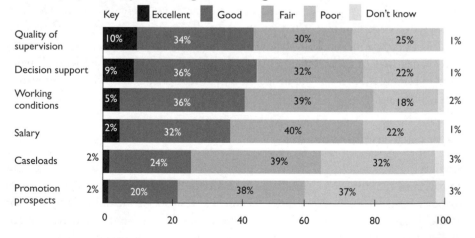

Source: Lombard, 2009b, p 16

In October of the same year the periodical reported a research finding from UNISON (the trade union to which social workers are most likely to belong, as local government employees) that more than a third of social workers in the south east of England were taking anti-depressants (McGregor, 2009). While in 2010 a survey of 600 social workers found 90% of respondents had caseload anxieties, with 10% of child protection workers and 22% of adult care workers having caseloads over 40, some with 70 to 80, and a few over 100 (Smith, 2010).

Yet, as the charts in Figure 2.1 appear to show, roughly three quarters of social workers seemed pretty satisfied with their jobs, and about the same proportions thought their working conditions were 'good' or 'fair', although there was some dissatisfaction with caseloads, and almost 40% of social workers felt they were 'stuck' in their organisations.

McLean (1999) examined the relationship between job satisfaction, stress and control over work in social services in more detail. He found significant levels of sickness absence and that time off work was linked to stress. However, this varied between different types of job and areas of work, with homecare workers in Northern Ireland reporting the lowest levels of stress, and child protection workers in inner London reporting the highest levels of stress. Workers with older people reported lower levels of stress than child and family workers. Residential workers in mental health and severe learning disabilities settings reported high levels of stress and also found night shifts stressful. Older research (Herzberg et al, 1959) identified job control as a correlate of reported job satisfaction, and this relationship held for social services staff, with field workers and homecare workers reporting relatively high levels of perceived autonomy. However, a second tranche of the research, following up one year later, after significant organisational change had occurred, found slightly lower levels of expressed control. This demonstrates a way in which the organisational setting impacts on how employees cope with stress arising from the nature of their work.

Job satisfaction and career pathways

Another way of exploring job stress and motivation in social work is to examine career pathways. Do the employment histories of social services staff suggest high turnover, burnout and job flight?

Andrew (1999) studied the employment histories of 2,031 social services staff in 11 local authorities in the UK. He found significant patterns of job change relating to age, gender, and the type of work within the sector (see Figure 2.2 and Table 2.1). Job change tends to tail off with age, with highest job mobility (average number of jobs 7.1) among the youngest workers in their twenties, considerable change (5.1 jobs on average) for workers in their thirties, reducing in their forties (2.9) to low levels of change for workers over 50 (2.1 jobs on the average). Men were more likely to make career moves, while women were more likely to be fitting work around their families. The highest turnover was amongst social work staff; the lowest turnover was amongst home care staff. Overall the patterns suggest that, once in social services at around age 30, workers had typically returned to or moved between jobs, with fieldworkers being most likely to move between authorities, and home care workers and residential workers being more likely to come and go from the same authority.

Figure 2.2: Average number of jobs held per decade of employment in social services for staff in England, Scotland and Northern Ireland

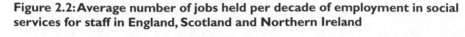

Source: Andrew, 1999, p 30

Table 2.1: Rate of past job turnover per decade by job type and age at first interview in England, Scotland and Northern Ireland

Turnover per decade	Job type	Base	n		Age	Base	n
Manager	3.8	204	467	Under 30	7.1*	154	189
Social work staff	4.6	345	470	30-39	5.1	463	620
Home care	2.7*	686	543	40-49	2.9	555	702
Residential	4.3	450	551	50+	2.1	505	513
All	3.6	1,685	2,031			1,677	2,024

* Job turnover was lower for home care workers and older members of staff. Significant at $p < 0.05$, controlling for gender and regional variations.

Source: Andrew, 1999, p 31

It should be noted that the research from which this snapshot is drawn was a Department of Health-funded survey of the social care workforce, initiated in 1992 and carried out in 1994–95. This timing meant that it coincided with the introduction of changes to social services organisation arising from the NHS and Community Care Act 1990 and the Children Act 1989. Consequently the findings regarding the motivation of social workers cannot be entirely separated from the sweeping organisational changes of the period, a contingency that the authors acknowledge. But, with those caveats in mind, what can this research reveal about motivation in social services? The expressed high levels of work satisfaction of homecare workers may reflect the relative ease with which this work can be fitted around family responsibilities. There is also evidence that job change is fairly normal within social services, and that those who leave social services employment often return. Perhaps this supports the view of social services work as an emotional, particularly stressful kind of work from which workers need a change from time to time but do not necessarily want to abandon altogether. This could also suggest that social workers' motivation is substantially linked to the intrinsic satisfaction of the work, rather than to its material rewards. However, as Andrew (1999) speculates, it might also mean that organisational development and opportunities for progression were not available, so workers looked elsewhere.

Robbins (1993) takes the approach of looking at the relationship between job satisfaction and organisational structure. In this view, the strategy of management to a large extent determines the structure of the organisation, and this in turn has a major influence upon whether the front-line worker is, or is not, happy in his or her job. For example, Robbins notes that, in a traditional, hierarchical bureaucracy, a high degree of job specialisation is called for. This means that front-line jobs can be narrowly defined, closely hedged with rules, procedures and instructions, and repetitive. Front-line, desk-bound administrative roles in social services offices can sometimes have this character. While an employee with a 'job-and-finish', '9 to 5' orientation to work may express a degree of job satisfaction in such an organisational structure, an employee with a career orientation, wanting personal development opportunities and a more creative, discretionary role, is likely to express low job satisfaction. Additionally, since hierarchical bureaucracies create resilient boundaries between departments and these (departments) tend to be inward looking, networking opportunities may be restricted. A flatter, more flexible organisational structure, characterised by adaptable duties, informal communication, and decentred decision-making authority, may offer low job satisfaction to an employee who thrives on direct management, routine and a steady workload. Conversely, such an organisational structure may provide high job satisfaction for the employee who likes to network and self-manage.

This possible explanation of motivation in terms of satisfaction and opportunities provided by organisational structure will be considered later in this chapter when we look at the work of Kanter (1977), who also considered the specific gender dimensions.

Classic theories of motivation

Motivation (as well as other areas of the study of organisational behaviour, such as leadership, groups, communication and decision making) was a core element of organisational behaviour in the first half of the twentieth century. Motivation appears in classic works such as those of Simey (1937), Simon (1945), Barnard (1948) and Simon et al, 1950), where there appears a quite natural relationship between these areas of study and the needs and interests of the manager.

Despite management bias in older textbooks, observations of much wider significance are frequently made. Barnard (1948), for example, although head of a large corporation, voluntarily administered unemployment relief for a while in the 1930s, and understood that organisations were not just about economic needs but fulfilled other human needs too, such as the need to do something worthwhile or, indeed, just to do something. This accords with more recent views such as those of Simon and Burns (1997) on Baltimore inner city gangs, from which it emerged that, even when alternative sources of economic support existed, some people still had a strong need to be part of an organisation and would gravitate back to the gang organisation to meet this need. The classic pieces of motivation research traditionally included in mainstream organisational behaviour textbooks (such as Buchanan and Huczynski, 2004) often have something to say of relevance to social work, even if indirectly: specifically, the work of the researchers Mayo (1933), McClelland et al (1953), Herzberg et al (1959) and Vroom (1964), who will be discussed in turn below.

Mayo: work psychology

The research of Elton Mayo (1933) in the 1920s marked a decisive break with the utilitarian thinking that had dominated the factory age. Mayo replaced the health-and-efficiency approach, characteristic of the period prior to the First World War (see **Chapter One**), with something new: work psychology. Mayo appears to have begun with the intention of studying the impact of lighting conditions upon work output, but, after manipulating these with limited effect, he abruptly changed direction. Mayo did also systematically vary work breaks, work group size and incentives, and analyse the results, but he is not remembered for this so much as for his exploration of women's and men's feelings about their work. Instead of the input-output 'black box' research model, he moved to using a non-directive interviewing technique with his subjects, a technique he had come across in another context and been fascinated by. The non-directive interviewing method had been used to look for psychological disturbance, as Mayo knew, but his own use of it with 'A1' employees was a relatively new departure. The result was a large amount of data that he subjected to content analysis, identifying work-related themes. The richness of the findings perhaps explains why no obvious or simple conclusions were drawn, and also explains why subsequent attempts to pigeon-hole Mayo have failed. In his research, women in particular talked about the supervisory relationship, the working group and doing satisfying work, and this makes his work the ancestor of contemporary debate about motivation in social work and its relation to organisational setting.

Figure 2.3, taken from Mayo (1933), illustrates his work very well. Although all items in the content analysis of Mayo's interview statements rest upon individual perceptions of the significance of things, such as 'noise' and 'dirt' for instance, items such as job interest, supervision and social contact clearly have a strong subjective element, making the analysis of these statements extremely resistant to quantitative analysis. The column on the left records the degree of variation in workers' comments.

Figure 2.3: Mayo's research data from *The human problems of an industrial civilization*

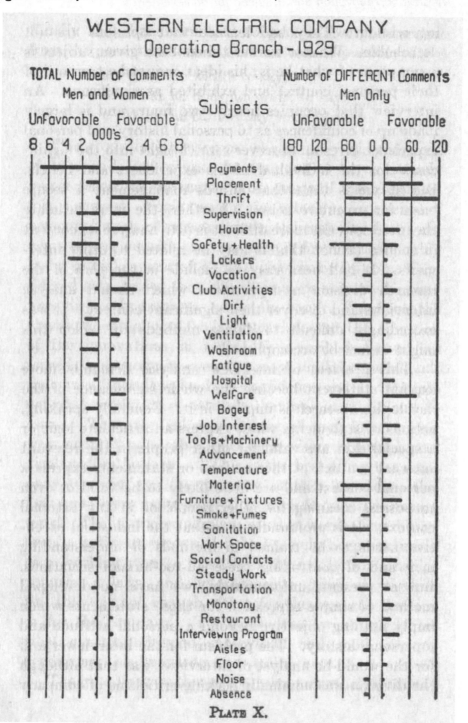

Source: Mayo 1933, p 90.

McClelland: motivation and the need for achievement

David McClelland was an American psychologist who developed a theory that work motivation is acquired in early experience (McClelland et al, 1953) and, in some respects, this is a theory that should therefore appeal to social workers. McClelland stated that 'too little is known about the processes of personality change at relatively complex levels' (McClelland, 1965, p 321), noting that empirical study of the problem is hampered by both practical and theoretical difficulties. His conclusion, however, was that motives are learned early; they are 'affectively toned associative networks' arranged in a hierarchy of strength, within a given individual. His 'need achievement' (or *n*–achievement) theory outlined sources of *n*–achievement as:

1. Parents who encouraged independence in childhood
2. Praise and rewards for success
3. Association of achievement with positive feelings
4. Association of achievement with one's own competence and effort, not luck
5. A desire to be effective or challenged
6. Intrapersonal strength.

Mothers were argued to hold the ultimate responsibility for the work motivation of their children, although adults could be re-equipped and McClelland developed short courses to develop achievement motivation.

As per point 5 above, 'Need for Achievement' is also related to the difficulty of tasks people choose to undertake: those with low *n*–achievement preferring easy tasks or very difficult tasks (in which failure might be expected); those with high *n*–achievement choosing tasks that are challenging but achievable and therefore rewarding.

Herzberg: Motivation–Hygiene theory

Herzberg et al (1959) and Vroom (1964) are cited as illustrations of 1950s research into work motivation in most textbooks of organisational behaviour, and it is Herzberg's focus upon level of job responsibility and personal growth that is of interest from a social work point of view. Herzberg's Motivation–Hygiene theory states that people are influenced by two sets of factors. 'Motivational' factors include:

- achievement;
- recognition;
- the work itself;
- levels of responsibility;
- promotion; and
- personal growth.

The 'Hygiene' factors are those which result in dissatisfaction if lacking and are:

- pay and benefits;
- company policies and the organisation;
- relationships with colleagues; and
- supervision.

It is commonly written of this research that it reflects a now lost era of full employment, and its findings are therefore criticised as being of limited contemporary use. However, Herzberg himself was the first to reflect upon this, dismissing it with the observation that fluctuations in the economy did not of themselves invalidate his findings, which he came to see as a window upon human nature.

Vroom: expectancy theory

Victor Vroom's (1964) expectancy theory states that motivation is what governs the choices that an individual makes based on expected results. In other words, people are motivated by whether or not they feel the eventual outcome is worth the effort. His work, usefully, notes the characteristically female composition of social work and some other professions, suggesting that this type of work draws on a putatively female motivation of caring for others.

We begin, then, from the classical literature of organisational behaviour to get an outline of the specific motivation of social workers. Taking Vroom and McClelland together, we can begin to glimpse the outlines of a familiar theory of gender socialisation and carer motivation, noting that this is from a male point of view. It is difficult to resist the conclusion that the organisational behaviour theories of work motivation are a male window upon 'motivation'. In the summary of his late 1940s research on achievement motivation, McClelland (1987) acknowledged that he was studying just *one* motive: there are other motives, such as the motive to care for others. In sum, these models of work motivation could be used to understand social workers in social work organisations, but only if they were developed to include the dimensions of motivation appropriate to such work.

Motivations in social work

Doing meaningful work

In the early 1970s Pearson (1973) examined the changing motivation of social workers, asking 'Why do they do it?'. Pearson found that his social work students often wanted to do social work partly because they saw it as the expression of a morally superior, critical attitude towards the *status quo*, and partly because they saw it as meaningful work as opposed to perceived 'acquisitive' work (ie that in the private sector). To this extent, social workers put themselves in a slightly marginal position in relation to mainstream society (Uttley, 1981). Although Pearson was primarily concerned with what he saw as a 'cop out', 'privatised' solution to essentially public and political problems in society, his work raised a key question about the motives of social workers: that of its perceived ethical status. Pearson's work prompted a string of research about motivation in social work and this question remained a useful one in follow-up studies in the 1980s, when it was found that, despite a more 'privatised', personal growth orientation, students of social work still perceived it to be an ethical choice (O'Connor et al, 1984), such motivation even crossing national boundaries (Uttley, 1981). In the 1990s, Solas (1994) detected an incipient instrumentalism, yet, when Furness and Gilligan (2006) followed up in the 2000s, they found that bursary support was less important to students than the ethical character of the work.

Religious and faith-based motivations

To what extent can religious motivation be considered a significant factor in the work motivation of social workers? Furness and Gilligan (2010) note that in Britain, and indeed elsewhere, faith-based social work and social care agencies provide cover in substantial areas of provision (they give the figure of 15% of the national caseload). While it cannot be straightforwardly assumed that everyone working in such organisations necessarily shares the faith perspective of the organisation, the persisting identity of these organisations and their usually unambiguous faith-based mission statements make it reasonable to infer at least a sympathetic attitude of most of the workforce to the religious orientation of their organisation. In addition, the

Octavia Hill

religious motivation of such founders of social work as Mary Richmond and Octavia Hill is proverbial, as is that of many of its exemplars in each generation since then. When interviewing applicants for one of the first British university-based welfare work courses, Agatha Harrison complained that:

> "I am still faced with people whose reason for entering this work is their successful handling of a Sunday School class." (Harrison, 1956, p 25)

Harrison herself was questioned, she said, by the Young Women's Christian Association about her religious observance before she was sent to do welfare work in China in the 1920s, an instance which illustrates the context of social work at that time.

Timms (1970) has challenged this image of the ubiquity of religious motivation in social work. He argued that the Victorian pioneers of social work were, in fact, typically substituting organised action for religiously motivated charitable giving. As we have seen in the Introduction to this book, this assertion was part of Timms' wider project of recognising the discontinuities in social work history, in order to free social work from the perceived 'dead hand' of Victorian attitudes concerning the deserving poor, and from stereotyped assumptions regarding the motivation of social workers. Nonetheless, given the spread of provision by faith-based organisations in all areas of social work, faith continues to be an important marker of motivation in the profession. In an earlier study, Furness and Gilligan (2006) surveyed social work students and practitioners and found that the latter were more likely to consider faith-sensitive, or faith-related, interventions appropriate than were the former, although they also found some variation according to faith background.

The motivation of women and men in social work

Wilson (1996) has pointed out that, on some dimensions, women's motivation appears to differ from that of men. In particular, women tend to internalise failure whereas men externalise it, and to externalise success whereas men internalise it. Female social workers are therefore more likely than their male colleagues to see promotional failure as their own fault and be less likely to look elsewhere for better opportunities. As noted above, social care work may appeal to women because it is a form of working that can often be structured around family caring hours. However, women without family caring responsibilities are more likely to approximate the labour market participation of men (Jensen et al, 2000), and Wilson (1996) noted that as managers women showed very similar motivational patterns to men.

In **Chapter Three** on communication in organisations, the different communication styles of men and women are outlined, together with discussion about the role this may play in deterring men from caring work in general, and from social work in particular. But some men *are* motivated to join a predominantly female occupation, so what is the motivation of men to enter social work?

Lupton (2006) interviewed 27 men in predominantly female occupations such as librarianship, junior school teaching and nursing, to ascertain their reasons for entering their jobs. Lupton found that a variety of motivations were given, ranging from careerism to just 'drifting' into the job. He observed that men typically do not stay in social work and that their presence is on a 'revolving door' basis, but he regarded this as a non-explanation, in motivational and organisational terms. Interestingly, Lupton settled upon an explanation in terms of social class. There is no evidence that men in social work organisations come from any particular social class or minority ethnic background (Simpson, 2005). Men's motivations for entering predominantly female occupations such as social work appear to be a complex mix of later life career choice, 'glass escalator' careerism, preference for non-profit public sector employment, a lack of success in or aversion to the competitive environment of male occupations and organisations, and a personal disposition towards care work.

It is interesting to note that Lupton (2006) found that the men in predominantly female occupations such as social work admitted to sometimes lying about their occupations when in the company of other men. Lupton's respondents seem to have felt some discomfort about the masculinity of their occupations, with some using activities such as DIY and sport to reassert their masculinity, implying that this counterbalanced de-motivating aspects of working in 'female' jobs and organisational settings. Overall this may suggest that their motivation to enter social work was attenuated by other negative associations that came with the job.

Individual versus organisational motivations

Practice example: intrinsic and extrinsic motivation

In the central social services area office in Milltown, duty social work cover for all services is run from the same small room. In this room, two desks face each other: on one side, a duty worker intercepts child and family emergencies and enquiries, while on the other side, a worker intercepts all adult services walk-ins, telephone enquiries and emergencies.

Jeanette Mohammed begins her shift on the duty desk to find that her opposite number, Kyril, is sitting with his feet on the desk reading a newspaper. They exchange greetings cordially and the day proceeds with a series of telephone reports and enquiries on her side of the office and a series of walk-in customers for Kyril. Both work hard, but Jeanette finds that by the end of the shift she still has much unfinished work to do, most of it on referrals and enquiries from earlier in the day. Kyril, however, has his briefcase on his desk and is looking repeatedly at his watch, clearly ready to go home. Jeanette has a sense of injustice about this, but feels she cannot mention it to Kyril, who seems blameless. She decides to share her feeling of injustice and frustration with her supervisor during her next supervision session.

In supervision, Jeanette describes the situation and her feelings, without identifying her fellow worker. Her supervisor, however, recognises the behaviour immediately, and nods to show that she knows who the worker is. She explains that Kyril is an efficient worker who manages his workload very effectively. If a customer is not eligible for services provided by the Department, he tells them so immediately and moves on to the next customer as quickly as possible, with politeness. Jeanette, however, feels that she is in the job to help people and often finds herself spending long periods listening to people's problems and absorbing their distress. The supervisor tells Jeanette that she cannot help everybody.

A picture begins to emerge of social work as caring work which attracts women in particular, which has a relatively high ethical valuation, which often attracts those from religious backgrounds even if they are not practising themselves, and which requires a degree of independent or even critical thinking. These motivations, as Jeanette describes in the case study, are 'personal' rather than organisational factors. It is interesting to note that, when asked about motivation and social work, practitioners will sometimes refer to personal biographical factors (Morales, 2009). This is in contrast with reporting in the press media about *de*-motivating which typically focuses on factors outside of the individual, such as heavy workload, poor supervision, high pressure, and the climate of public opinion. Overall, theories of work motivation tend to acknowledge some mix of 'external', or perceived rewards, and 'internal', or psychological drive factors. Wright's (1991) related distinction, between Content and Process theories of work motivation, traces back to the philosopher Locke a division between expectation of the results of action, on one hand, and individual need, on the other. It is arguable that an emphasis on one or other of these approaches characterises particular theories and concepts of work motivation, and even particular theoretical trends over time.

Individual motivations

A classic study of workplace motivation was conducted in the US armed forces by Stouffer et al (1952). The researchers in this wartime study asked comparatively new recruits to the US Military Police and to the US Air Cadets what they thought their promotion prospects were. They found contentedness with promotion opportunities to be independent of actual opportunities and of comparisons with other areas of the military. Instead, subjects compared themselves with others they knew in the same unit. This was seen as a psychological reflex. More educated subjects tended to be more dissatisfied, again suggesting individual factors as an explanation for observed differences in behaviour within the same organisation.

Murray's Thematic Apperception Test: psychodynamic techniques and motivation

The Thematic Apperception Test (TAT) was developed in the 1930s by American psychologists Henry A. Murray and Christiana D. Morgan to explore aspects of personality, including motivation (Murray, 1938). Murray used Harvard students as his subjects. He describes a number of similar tests for exploring the deep-lying or unconscious needs of subjects, and the book contains a title page acknowledgement that Freud's work provided the major working hypothesis of his researches, once again linking the histories of social work and organisational behaviour. Other tests he studied in the development of the TAT included ink-blot tests and a dramatic projection technique, based upon a study of children's play.

The TAT has been used in organisational behaviour research, for example by McClelland et al (1953) (as discussed earlier in this chapter). When we attempt to dredge the depths of individual work motivation with techniques such as these, we are likely to find unfulfilled desires, searches for identity and searches for meaning as motivating factors. This is not so very surprising, given that the subjects Murray (and others) used were people who expected their professional lives to meet these needs.

Kanter: motivation, opportunity and power

Such individual, psychological explanations for motivation persisted until the 1960s, until Kanter's (1977) exploration of opportunity, power and social composition of the organisation, particularly in relation to the motivation of women and men. Kanter outlined an additional dimension to the 'psychological factors' type of approach to motivation as seen above in the Stouffer et al (1952) study. He maintained that an important factor was organisational position and the opportunities linked to it, which led to opportunity-driven behaviours.

Those with lots of opportunities tend to make work the centre of their lives, over-value their abilities, identify with the organisation, be competitive, compare themselves to those who have done well, create informal action groups (which in social work could be equated to networking), protest and assert at work, and make use of the opportunities for training and personal growth, but become quickly disaffected if they do not move up within the organisation.

People with limited opportunities in their work organisations tend to limit their aspirations, have lower self-esteem, undervalue themselves, seek satisfaction outside work, dream of escape, have interrupted career patterns, tend to compare themselves only with their peers, are critical of management, tend to be griping, or soldiering, and are unlikely to protest at work. They display peer group loyalty, sometimes even to the extent of discouraging the mobility of others; tend to find worth through personal relationships; suffer parochiality (such as being tied to a particular residential unit); and have an instrumental orientation to work.

These motivational differences brought about by differential organisational opportunities, Kanter argued, not only had consequences for the work attitude of the individuals concerned, but also for those with whom they worked. For, those with limited opportunities and power tend to supervise others too closely, restricting their opportunities for growth and development, assessing their own status in relation to subordinates instead of those above, and are controlling and critical. They also tend to be territorial, reticent in meetings, and disliked. We may know social work colleagues like this: relatively powerless people with limited opportunities within their organisations for personal growth and development, who are perhaps too controlling of clients and reluctant to involve and support junior colleagues. The powerful are often the opposite: self-secure 'light touch' managers, confident and empowering social workers.

Kanter's third dimension of organisational behaviour is minority status, and this too has implications for motivation theory. If you feel you are in a minority, you are more likely to try to conform and will feel your mistakes are more visible, your credibility lower, your marginality higher, and your exclusion from peer networks greater. You will also tend to fall back on old friendships, have fewer upward opportunities as a consequence, and face more personal stress, finding self-presentation more difficult. Conversely, the theory predicts that members of majorities will tend to network more, learn the ropes, have ease in self-presentation, find credibility easier and less stressful, and, at the end of it, be more likely to move to higher status jobs.

However, Kanter observed that these factors are difficult to isolate empirically, that they overlap and, crucially, that they can only be interrupted from outside of these 'self-sealing systems', that is, by an organisation restructure, or by a move to another organisation. The implication of Kanter's work is that individuals need to create opportunities in their own working lives, and that organisations can facilitate this to a greater or lesser extent, with corresponding benefits to the organisation's objectives.

Reflective point: Think about how you could improve opportunities and power structures in the workplace?

You could move to an organisation that provides opportunities in different ways such as:

- job redesign or rotation
- new job ladders
- job description and performance appraisal
- career review
- open recruitment
- project management and the creation of temporary teams for specific tasks
- diffused management
- empowerment
- a flat organisational structure
- sponsorship
- mentoring for all employees.

Postmodern theories of motivation

Jackson and Carter (2000) argue that, while incentive theories of motivation probably 'read off' needs that are largely socially constructed in nature, the self by contrast is linked to deep-lying and hidden desires that are not accessible to others. This leads Jackson and Carter to conclude that it is not possible for one person to motivate another. There is perhaps a fundamental truth in this, insofar as an individual's desires can never be met by someone whose own subjectivity necessarily enters into the equation. This somewhat bleak picture of human relationships is mitigated by the acknowledgement that this is not necessarily an obstacle to individuals working to improve organisations or society more generally, which is fundamental to motivations in social work.

Yet Jackson and Carter assert that, although individuals cannot be motivated by other individuals, organisations can demotivate individuals; for example, by making a worker redundant, organisations can affect the valuation placed upon the self. Overall, however, they take the view that motivation to work is a 'non-issue'

(2000, p 156). This seems a pity, since we had begun, with Kanter's (1977) work, to understand work motivation in terms of opportunities and organisational position, an approach which held out the possibility of more satisfying careers, for women in particular. Perhaps the litmus test of these theories would be an organisation based upon Kanter's approach, that is, a social work career that moves beyond a series of salary-linked professional development milestones, to one which will result in more fulfilled workers and improved staff retention and motivation.

Conclusion

In this chapter several approaches to the motivation of social workers have been considered. Some approaches have examined the intrinsic rewards of the work itself, and these were referred to in the survey of social workers themselves. We found that there might be a gendered dimension to perceived intrinsic reward, when men's motivation to enter social work was considered. The historical and cultural background of religious motivation in social work was briefly discussed, along with its continuing relevance in social work. Other approaches looked to the personal development needs of social workers, and from these to the organisation's structure of reward, advancement, and personal development opportunities. A third approach dropped the assumption that social workers themselves actually know why they like the job; instead, unconscious motivations were sought. A related approach explored the view that social workers want, like everyone else, things which are missing from their lives, and this led to the rather bleak view that work is a search for substitute satisfactions. Finally, postmodern approaches were briefly considered, together with their implication that motivation is unique, private, and perhaps ultimately ineffable.

It would be remiss to end this chapter without once again noting the practical overlapping of motivation in social work organisations with virtually every other area of organisational behaviour: culture, organisational change, management style, decision making and communication all affect individual motivation and are in turn dependent upon it.

▶KEY LEARNING POINTS

- Motivation and job satisfaction are not necessarily linked to stress
- Classic theories of motivation can be applied to social work, but do not take account of motivations particular to social work and caring work
- Motivation in social work may be gendered, although traditional theories of motivation implicitly generalise male assumptions
- The organisation is a primary source of motivation (and demotivation) for individual social workers, despite an emphasis upon intrinsic reward and vocationalism

- There are links between minority status (within an organisation) and motivation, and this has implications for anti-oppressive practice

▶EXERCISE: IDENTIFYING INTERPERSONAL MOTIVATORS

With a friend, discuss the ways in which you motivate others from day to day. In particular, identify the specific rewards you use such as smiles, hugs, praise, money, and so on. Identify two rewards which each of you finds particularly effective. Arrange to both keep one day's record of your use of these motivators. At your next, follow-up meeting, compare results. What overall theories of motivation might explain the relative success of the rewards you each used? (Adapted from Frantzve, 1983, pp 54-6.)

CHAPTER THREE

Communication: does the social work grapevine work for you?

What you will learn in this chapter
- An understanding of directions of communication and communication roles
- Obstacles to effective communication
- Informal routes of communication, such as grapevines
- Gender is important in understanding communication within social work organisations
- The importance of communication in the supervisory relationship
- Communication with clients is also influenced by the organisation

Introduction

The aim of this chapter is to bridge the gap between the social–psychological theories of interpersonal communication that appear in other areas of social work training and the organisational theories of information pathways, barriers and obstacles, 'gangplanks' between organisations and process re-engineering models which will be discussed later in this book.

Although there has been some excellent research on the impact of the physical environment upon communication, since the work of Rogers (1951) and Biestek (1961) we have tended to see communication in social work as primarily a matter of interpersonal skills. There is much truth in this of course, but this chapter will show that communication in organisations between individuals, including between social workers and service users, is also affected by the organisation and its structure.

The well-travelled letter

A social worker arrived at work in his social work team one morning to find a rather battered letter in his in-tray. The envelope had been written upon in many different hands, and in different coloured inks; it had evidently passed through many hands before coming to rest in his in-tray. The first recipient, according to the envelope, was HRH the Queen, the next was the Prime Minister. After that, in order: the Secretary of State for Health; the minister for local government; the social worker's director of social services; the director of services to adults; the area manager of adults' services; the social worker's line manager; and finally the social worker himself whose name lay near one edge of the envelope. When he opened the letter, he found it was a request for assistance from a service user.

The laborious route of this simple written communication illustrates that the obstacles to effective communication in social work cannot be entirely removed by improving our listening skills, building a relationship of trust with the client and controlling our paralanguage. The positive thoughts in the social worker's mind that morning were probably that the system had in fact worked for the service user: after all, the message eventually resulted in the provision of services. If there were misgivings, they were likely to have been about the valuable time of many busy people that had been consumed in the process, when the majority of them were not themselves in a position to visit the service user or to arrange the services. Could a more efficient route have been taken?

Directions of communication

Centralised and decentralised communication

The case study above also highlights the difference between centralised and decentralised communication systems in organisations (Vecchio, 2000). Centralised systems are efficient for routine tasks, whereas decentralised systems are best for complex tasks. Whether or not there exist any 'routine' social work tasks is not such an easy question as it might at first sight appear, since the most 'routine' service user contact has the potential for complexity. Service user transport is an example of a centralised system, in some local authority social services departments at least. Homecare is also usually a centralised system (although perhaps it should not be). The extent to which these services are commissioned directly or indirectly by service users from private providers will also be a factor here.

Centralised systems can create leaders, but using decentralised working can stop this (Shaw, 1976). For example, in case allocation, if one person in a self-managing team has a monopoly of case allocation, they might effectively push themselves into a management position. The result of this may be reduced job satisfaction for the rest of the team (Shaw, 1976).

Vertical and horizontal communication

Another way of looking at communication in organisations is in terms of vertical and horizontal communication. In vertical communication, top-down communication tends to consist of policies and mission statements from senior management. These are commonly, but not always, viewed by those who receive them as feedback upon the behaviour of other organisational players, including themselves; often as criticism. Consider, for example, the impact of briefing memoranda on alcohol policy, or on return-to-work interviews for practitioners in the workplace. Viewing such missives as criticism actually presupposes an upward flow of information in the organisation equal to that coming down, a fact which research stubbornly refuses to ratify (Buchanan and Huczynski, 2004). The motives of top-down communications appear to be a magnet for distortion, for example, one student on placement reported a policy statement about paternity leave being explained thus: "They did it to spite single mums – the Director's wife has just left him".

Upward communication, on the other hand, tends to consist of progress reports, statistical returns and only occasionally of reactions to work issues. Reasons for this paucity of upward feedback may include:

- a fear of 'card-marking' for the next round of redundancies (see also discussion of 'watch your back' cultures in **Chapter Six**);
- feedback is felt to be futile; or
- people are just too busy to spend time offering upward feedback that has not been requested.

Another difference between the two flows of vertical communication in organisations is that managers expect prompt responses, but employees generally do not. Overall, employees get less feedback on organisational behaviour than they would like (Buchanan and Huczynski, 2004). Distortion occurs here too, and downward communication is not always quicker, as the example of the service user's letter to the Queen demonstrated.

In 'horizontal' communication, 'gangplanks' are sometimes necessary. A gangplank is a direct communication route to an equivalent-level worker in another organisation or service unit, which avoids the round-the-houses communication pathway of centralised communication. For example, the Care Manager has the equivalent-level Occupational Therapist's telephone number or email, but may not have a 'gangplank' to other people in that department and may have to go through the hierarchy. An alternative gangplank might be walking down the corridor and speaking to the contact in person. Gangplanks are particularly important in multidisciplinary working.

Practice example: 'silo' departments and multidisciplinary teams

Jean Harlow, a very experienced youth worker, took up her first post-qualifying appointment in a Child and Adolescent Mental Health Services (CAMHS) setting. At interview, the panel were particularly impressed by her pre-qualifying experience and she felt sure she could make a valuable contribution to the multidisciplinary setting. During her induction period she settled into a small but bright office on her own, flanked by offices up and down the corridor containing team members specialising in psychiatry, family therapy and psychology. Jean was introduced to all of her colleagues during induction and they showed warmth and genuine appreciation of her arrival in the team.

As the weeks went by, however, Jean began to feel increasingly isolated in her office. She managed her caseload well and made appropriate referrals to colleagues, but the kind of team working she had previously been used to in an open-plan office was missing. She began to feel mildly depressed and even wondered if she had chosen the wrong job.

One morning she decided it was up to her to do something about the situation. She planned a lunch, informed colleagues, bought snacks, placed notices in the corridor, propped her door open and hovered in the corridor to make sure she didn't miss passers-by. Jean found that this self-promotion was more effective in getting her name and expertise circulated to her immediate neighbours than the induction had been, to the extent that they continued to 'drop in' at lunchtimes.

Communication roles

In the directional views of communication in organisations outlined above, it is already possible to identify specific communication roles. For example, there are 'gatekeepers', such as personal assistants, and 'liaisons', such as National Health Service hospital discharge coordinators. There are also communication 'isolates': beware of Meals on Wheels operators who are uninformed of service user holidays. Younger, newer or marginal, part-time workers are more likely to be communication isolates than their full-time, permanent, long-service equivalents, and this is an important factor to be taken into consideration when social work duty rotas are under construction. This may be especially important given the trend towards agency and part-time staff appointments in social services (Lombard, 2009b).

There are also communication 'cosmopolites', who know and network with lots of people across several organisations. An example might be a colleague in the press office; the director's PA is probably a cosmopolite, too, as well as the payroll clerk, or the trade union steward.

Knowing the communication roles of colleagues and understanding informal 'gangplanks' or formal communication channels is indispensable organisational knowledge for the social worker in his or her first encounter with the social service organisation. It is now appropriate to consider some of the barriers to communication that she or he will also encounter.

Barriers to communication

Overload

 One oft-cited barrier to effective communication is information overload: there is simply too much detail that needs to be processed in-depth, or that does not need to be processed at all (Handy, 1993; Kakabadse et al, 2005). For example, when covering the cases of an absent colleague, even if she has only slipped out of the office for a moment, to respond appropriately to her distressed client on the telephone, you may have to wade through a mass of case information. While in supervision the supervisor does not

need to know all the details of all of your cases. Telephone calls from clients can contain a mass of information, not all of which is relevant, so it is important to be directive, in order to circumvent that barrier to effective communication (Koprowska, 2005). There is the alternative theory to this that time pressure is the barrier and the meandering communication of the service user does contain information that the social worker may need to know but does not have time to hear (Lishman, 1994).

Time pressures can indeed be an obstacle to communication and this is nowhere more obvious than in supervision (Hawkins and Shohet, 2006). Morrison (2001) identifies several reasons given for avoiding discussion of stress and time pressures within supervision, such as a culture of secrecy about showing feelings and helplessness (no one else is complaining; what can *I* do?). Strategies for avoiding discussion of stress and overload in supervision include retraction ("I just had a bad day"), going off sick, or even resigning. The communication aspects of supervision will be explored in more detail later in this chapter.

Organisational culture

As noted above, an organisational culture can influence channels of communication. A culture of suspicion can impact negatively upon communication. If mistrust is the norm in the organisation, internal messages may be over-examined to look for hidden implications for the recipient, while a fear of the potentially public character of emails can inhibit open and effective communication.

Different organisational settings of can have very different communication styles, and this is a particular problem in social work. Gould (1998) discussed social work organisations as learning organisations and noted that some organisations, for example those with a medical remit, tended to be more hierarchical in communication structure and that this affected communication patterns, which in turn affected the successful implementation of learning organisation changes. Communication between employees of differing rank could be obstructed by invisible barriers of rank; put bluntly, subordinates feel inhibited in what they can or cannot say to a senior colleague, and *vice versa*. Such barriers prevent the free flow of information that is considered necessary in a learning organisation, and such obstacles can impinge upon the outcomes for service users of the organisation. Gould (1998) identified a second type of organisation structure in which authority was decentred and management flatter, a sort of diffused-authority network, and argued that communication was less inhibited in such an organisation. Such an organisation was therefore more likely to be a 'learning' organisation in which new knowledge and skills spread quickly, enabling a more rapid response to service user need.

Informal communication and the grapevine

The formal models of communication in organisations tend to refer to 'chain of command' hierarchical flows, or variations upon them. Even structuring teams around the information pathways through organisations or buildings furnishes an essentially formal model of communication. If actual information flows in the sense of who talks to whom (Parsons and Bales, 1956) are studied, a grapevine 'map' is the result (Davis, 1953). Some research supports the view that grapevine information is typically distorted, but is the main source of employee information on controversial subjects. Why do people participate enthusiastically in grapevines? Perhaps they do so because it enables them to believe that others see them as 'in-the-know'. One of the earliest pieces of research on grapevine communication which may shed some light upon this question was that conducted by Caplow (1946-7; see Sutton and Porter, 1968), which looked at the transmission of regimental rumours in the US army. Caplow appears to have identified a few 'Sergeant Bilko' characters (like the lead character in 1950s US comedy *The Phil Silvers Show*) who passed information between groups within the regiment, but later research by Davis (1953) failed to replicate this finding among executives in a manufacturing company. Davis (1953) tried to identify who passed various pieces of information between departments and found, interestingly, that there were no single manipulators of information; rather, diverse individuals sometimes passed on some of the information they knew and at other times did not. When Sutton

and Porter (1968) conducted a 'grapevine' study in a governmental organisation, they found their results matched neither Caplow's nor Davis's, although, like Davis, a loose group of shifting membership, which included about 10% of staff, was found to be passing information. For Sutton and Porter the information flows were primarily within departments rather than between departments, as was the case in the manufacturing company studied by Davis (1953). It is tempting to speculate that organisational structure (and possibly culture) is a factor in grapevine operation: in the army a few well-known 'Bilkos' will tell you what you want to know provided they identify you as a 'buddy' in the same regiment; in business accounts staff know what's happening in the sales office and may or may not talk about it. In local government, however, social workers are not really interested in what is happening in the environmental health department, but a loosely constituted group of individuals occasionally communicate the endlessly interesting activities of their own senior managers.

In his research on formal communication, Simon (1945) recognised the importance of informal grapevines, but found that they were gendered: with women being more likely to pass on information to other women but rarely to men.

The relationship between service users and informal communication networks is also important in social work. We may know from our own experience that service users will ask social workers and other social services staff if rumours that they have heard about social services are true. Vecchio (2000) states that it is sometimes better to correct rumours than ignore them.

Gender issues in communication

Communication differences

Newell (2001) argues that the mainstream model of communication used in organisational textbooks assumes a 'level playing field' of men talking to other men. Based on this assumption, obstacles to communication are presented as things such as departmental boundaries or individual prejudice. Newell notes, however, that men and women speak the same words but with sometimes subtly different meanings conveyed, so a more sophisticated analysis of organisational communication may be required if its gendered nature is to be fully understood.

It is widely argued that men and women communicate differently: from popular books, such as *Men are from Mars, women are from Venus* (Gray, 1992) which aim to help navigate the conflicting communication styles of men and women, to Butler's (1990) thesis that women perform communication in a different way, although Newell (2001) argues that communication itself constructs gender, and not the other way around. Either way, if the typical social work team is predominantly female this will alter the context of communication and may mean that communication in the team has 'female' characteristics. The organisation constructs and controls the teams within which individual social workers operate, so this is another way in which an organisational understanding of communication is helpful, rather than a purely skills-based approach.

As already noted in **Chapter Two**, men are much less likely than women to work in the caring professions (McLean, 2003). Men avoid this 'emotional labour' for two main reasons: first, because it is not perceived as skilled labour in the wider society (Payne, 2000); and second, because working-class men in particular do not perceive themselves as having the requisite patience and 'use of self' skills required by this work (Nixon, 2009). This 'emotional intelligence' is argued to be an essential core skill of social work (Howe, 2008) and is seen to be a more typically female attribute (Nixon, 2009). There is a debate about the ease with which (and extent to which) men can be trained in these 'emotional intelligence' skills (Goleman, 1995; Morrison, 2001).

Part of the argument about these core skills is that men do not routinely use language expressive of mood states, and do not explore the mood states of others. It is interesting in this connection to note that some of the most commercially successful ideas in coaching organisational communication can perhaps be seen as 'female' skills. Consider for example the phenomenal success of Booher's (1994) highly regarded communication training for organisations: in *Communicate with confidence*, Booher recommends behaviour as simple as showing an interest in the other person. Elementary perhaps, but it clearly cannot be taken for granted.

There is also a claim that women's interrogative forms of address are less oppressive than those used by men, because they are expressed through the use of provisional and tentative assertions. Women use tag questions at the end of statements, such as "won't we?" or "isn't it?" conveying uncertainty, whereas men typically use such questions less often (Lakoff, 2004). Lakoff identified these differences between women's and men's communication as the use of a specialised vocabulary: men have a vocabulary which they don't share with women, and *vice versa*. For example, 'empty' adjectives are used by women to convey an emotional reaction, such as, 'cuddly', 'yummy' and 'cute'. Men typically use stronger expletives than those used by women, while women use super-polite forms more frequently than men (Lakoff, 2004). Women also typically use a wider range of pitch and intonation than do men, and are more likely to use exaggerated expression, again conveying uncertainty.

Gender as an organisational barrier to communication

In her research into the organisational lives of secretaries, Kanter (1977) found that patrimonial authority relations were often a characteristic feature of their work. Weber distinguished characteristic features of patrimonial authority, arguing that the typically bureaucratic structure of the modern organisation is the antithesis of patrimonial feudalism, with characteristics of universalism, legalistic standards, specialisation and routinisation of tasks. However, Kanter argued that the transition between organisational forms is not complete, and that aspects of premodern forms persist in modern organisations, patrimony being one of these. Patrimony exists where loyalty and personal preference enter into relationships, into recruitment, work sharing, and, when personal informal communication largely takes the place of formal communication. Although this emphasis upon loyalty and a personal touch may appear harmless, it may lead to bias, to fragmentary paper trails, poor recording of decisions and unsatisfactory accountability audits.

Communication in social work supervision

For most social workers supervision is the most important relationship in the workplace (McLean, 1999). As previously highlighted, this relationship will also be gendered and Taylor (1994) has noted that the power and gender mix in the supervision relationship inevitably structures communication. There are other ways in which the organisation influences communication in supervision, for example, if the organisation has line managers who are themselves case-holding this may put pressure upon the manager's available time for supervision. Organisational culture can also significantly affect communication in supervision: consider, for example, the effects of a 'watch your back' culture in the organisation (see **Chapter Six**) upon openness or agenda-setting in supervision.

Wu and Hu (2009) researched supervisees and found that peer-group support had a significant effect upon the way in which supervision was perceived by the supervisee. In particular an abusive supervisory relationship was more likely to be perceived as such where peer group emotional support was strong. This should warn us against focusing too closely upon the supervision dyad or on negative and unhelpful individual behaviours in supervision (Gray et al, 2010), when considering typologies of the supervision models found in practice (Tsui, 2005).

A typology of negative behaviours in supervision can be found in Hawkins and Shohet (2000), who promote a 'learning organisation' model of supervision (see **Chapter Seven**). This supplements earlier models emphasising reflection and decision-making. They contrast this learning organisation model with several 'degenerate' forms of supervision, including:

- Hunt the personal pathology;
- Strive for bureaucratic efficiency;
- Watch your back;
- Driven by crisis; and
- The addictive organisation.

Each of these forms of 'degenerate' supervision imply generally problematic communication environments within the organisation, and so are worth looking at more closely here.

In a 'hunt the personal pathology' organisational culture, supervision is characterised by blaming and by the scapegoating of colleagues and of clients. Additionally in this model of supervision the supervision *itself* is perceived as being only for the untrained or needy; the implicit message being that if you make use of supervision it must be because you have a serious problem that you are unable to handle yourself or that you have made a serious mistake. If this attitude towards supervision exists within an organisation, the already reluctant supervisee may find herself breathing a sigh of relief when the supervisory session is cancelled, interrupted or cut short. Research done in children's homes (Berridge, 1985) has identified this view of supervision, which can lead us to wonder if this extends to the wider communication environment in some children's homes. Is it difficult to communicate about any kind of problem or mistake in such an environment?

In 'strive for bureaucratic efficiency' communication environments, supervision is characterised by high task orientation, low personal relatedness, problem-centred, mechanical checklist agendas, in which there is little about understanding or reflection. Although Hawkins and Shohet's (2000) findings were based on research done with nurses, social service workers will surely recognise this kind of communication environment, which is often a product of large individual caseloads and high-pressure management workloads; there simply is not time to cover the breaking crises, let alone step back and reflect upon strategy in individual cases. Consequently this communication form sometimes resembles 'driven by crisis' supervision, which is characterised by cancellation or postponement of supervision at the last minute, the low prioritisation of supervision compared to 'crisis work', and a communication environment in which having, or even manufacturing, a crisis is often the only way to get supervision. Clients may also react to this kind of communication environment; staff attention may be contingent upon clients 'acting out' in one way or another. Characteristically, discussions take place in an atmosphere of pressure.

'Watch your back' supervision can be part of a broader back-watching organisational culture. Supervision is characterised by dumping workloads and stress, a conspiratorial atmosphere, competition with other departments and a career orientation (especially in large organisations, such as the Civil Service). A typical indicator of this communication environment in social services is the use of organisational procedures to dump responsibility for individual cases onto other departments or service units. This is often accompanied by the avoidance of decision making and by characteristic recording practices in which decisions are buried in masses of detail or in correspondence between service units and departments (see **Chapters One** and **Four** for a discussion of the typical organisational structures and decision-making processes that accompany such communication practices).

Finally, Hawkins and Shohet (2000) refer to the communication style of the 'addictive organisation'. The key feature of this communication style is its indirectness. Social services employees will recognise the 'workaholic' culture accompanying this communication style, an organisational culture often centring around one key individual in a service unit or around a key manager in an area office. Here, the tacit assumption is that feelings should not be expressed openly; there is an emphasis upon being strong, good and right, even perfect, and above all unselfish. Collusion, rationalisation of dishonest or abusive behaviour, a 'don't rock the boat' damper on communication, a subtext of 'do as I say, not as I do', as well as a feeling that it is not acceptable to be playful, may all be present in this communication environment. Worst of all, management may be the first to collude with this model because it creates a hard-work culture. An interesting aspect of this type of communication environment is its resistance to 'outing', probably because it breeds indirectness and front-maintaining behaviours: colleagues are relatively easily drawn in by its appeal to loyalty and selflessness and often therefore collude with the culture. Unless a communication style can be identified, it can't be changed.

Stoltenberg and Delworth (1987) offer a developmental model of supervision, which also contains a developmental theory of interpersonal communication. Following a life-cycle approach outlined by Erikson (1980, 1994), Stoltenberg and Delworth envision the development of communication in supervision as a short series of stages, each with a specific problematic to be overcome or task to be accomplished. The model thus implies sequential order and growth. An advantage of this developmental approach to interpersonal communication in organisations is that it sees mistakes and failures as normal, while setting clear targets and giving participants a sense of progress and achievement. It is also therefore possible to start from an acceptance of where the supervisee is in skill terms. Disadvantages of the model are, first, that it tends to be normative, insofar as communication that does not develop according to the model can be interpreted as failure. Second, it can also be gender-blind. Taylor (1994) identifies sexist assumptions in supervision, for example the assumption that manipulativeness is a negative, 'female' practice to be eradicated, rather than a strategy of the powerless. Incidentally, although assertiveness training is usually included in chapters on power in organisational behaviour textbooks, it is arguably more appropriate to include it in a chapter on communication, because assertiveness training was based on the assumption that women's absence from senior management was about communication and that deficiencies in women's workplace socialisation needed to be compensated. This approach does not consider whether the power relationships permit women to exert their interpersonal influence.

Stoltenberg and Delworth's (1987) model has four stages, but what is interesting here is their ideal type of optimum communication in supervision. Here, the supervisee should be so good at supervision that she is able to supervise others herself; having overcome performance anxiety, over-professionalism and over-identification with the client, she accepts complexity and adapts to all levels and cultures, understanding the nature of power and gender in supervision and of course in communication generally. This is perhaps therefore a useful model for communication in social work organisations generally, not just for supervision.

Finally, a critical perspective on the perceived 'skill deficit' basis of models of this kind is offered by Engelbrecht (2010), who proposes a strengths-based approach to social work supervision. Engelbrecht acknowledges the inbuilt paternalism and problematising culture of traditional social work bureaucracies, and seeks to counter this – both in practice and in supervision – with a method built upon the assessment of existing skills, knowledge, service user knowledge and other strengths of the supervisee. The supervisor then identifies outcomes, based on these strengths, with the supervisee. This performance appraisal style structuring of communication in supervision has a refreshing 'positive regard' feel to it. However, as a pragmatic rather than theoretical approach to communication in supervision, this approach may be detached from any systematic understanding of organisational oppression within the supervision situation and might therefore fall prey to the individual bigotries and biases of the supervisor and their unconscious collusion in organisational oppression.

Communication in social work assessment

Of the various aspects of communication within and between social care organisations, it is surely the communication between the organisation and its customers that is the most important and characteristic of social work (Lishman, 1994). This communication is made up of paperwork and procedures on one hand and of the communication skills of the social worker on the other. The first are the formal system of communication of a bureaucracy (Simon, 1945); the second involve the performative skills of gender (Butler, 1990) as noted above.

Gray et al (2010) argue that communication in health and social care organisations must be fast, two-way, detailed, comprehensively networkable and, perhaps most important of all, must engage the customer fully. As noted above, this is not simply a matter of individual skills, the organisation influences communication between the social worker and her client just as it does communication between colleagues. Middleton (1997) argues that there is a potential mismatch between the organisational agenda and the practice of assessment. Middleton (1997) contends that, since the 1990s, the culture of the social services organisation has sometimes been more managerialist and less social work-professional, with the consequence that communication in assessment is potentially more time-limited than has been the case formerly. Rather than being 'fast, two-way and detailed' (Gray et al, 2010), social work communication could be viewed as a process which has slowed down access to services, deterring all but the most determined service users with a barrage of paperwork-driven communication (Middleton, 1997). This process-driven assessment approach could also be perceived as deskilling the social worker's communication, reducing the assessment to a series of protocols. These assertions are contentious, and will be considered in more detail in **Chapter Eleven** on organisational change.

Finally, Harlow and Lawler (2000) have argued that social work organisations typically have a normatively heterosexual communication environment, which tends to push to the margins issues of gay sexuality and relationships in the lives of service users. An example is the tendency for heterosexual relationships to be assumed within carers' assessments and in care plans. Clearly, this is an obstacle to good assessment and service provision.

Conclusion

Instead of asking how organisations can improve communication, we should perhaps ask how 'communication processes contribute to the maintenance of systems of domination' (Newell, 2001, p 81). Although there are a number of different theories about what can go wrong with communication in organisations, there is a surprising consensus about what good communication in welfare organisations should involve. As Lipsky (1980) found in his research on the bottom rungs of welfare bureaucracies, what people wanted was a communication environment in which one could admit mistakes and hear plain advice from colleagues freely and easily, and in which they could tell clients their own truth and hear theirs without obstruction.

Given, however, that a core function of communication in social work organisations is the communication of risk, there may have to be compromises in reconciling the increasingly specialised professional language of risk (Carson and Bain, 2008) with the desire for a service user-friendly, jargon-free communication environment.

> **▶KEY LEARNING POINTS**
>
> - Effective communication between colleagues can be impeded or facilitated by organisations
> - Understanding the direction of communication and communication roles can help facilitate better communication
> - Informal routes of communication, such as grapevines are significant in social work organisations
> - Reflecting on the impact of gender is important in understanding communication and the organisational context of communication
> - Communication can buttress or undermine systems of domination and oppression in organisations
> - Supervision is a significant communication relationship for which there are many different models of practice
> - Communication between social workers and service users is significantly affected by the structure and culture of the service delivery organisation

> **▶EXERCISE: REFLECTING ON YOUR SUPERVISION HISTORY**
>
> Split up into pairs or team up with a fellow student and take it in turns to examine your previous experiences of supervision. Try to establish where you are in your current supervision and what models of supervisory communication you have experienced.

CHAPTER FOUR

Decision making: do your practice decisions seem to make themselves?

Introduction

Reading old case files can sometimes give rise to the impression that no decisions were consciously made in a particular case or that, if a decision was made, it was not felt necessary to record it. Although, as Taylor (2010) has pointed out, social workers may be called upon to show that they have arrived at a 'reasonable' decision from a legal point of view, perhaps the recording social worker felt that someone else made the all-important resource decisions, or that the decision to provide services was somehow an inexorable outcome of the assessment process, and it was therefore not necessary or appropriate to record a decision. Yet, reading contemporary electronic files in which a decision or outcome is required by the format can give the converse impression that, although a decision is recorded, no real choice was evident in the process.

When looking at decisions from the perspective of the organisational it is important to note that decision making is equated with the locus of power to which we will return in **Chapter Ten**. In terms of organisational behaviour the problem of unsatisfactory decision making becomes a wider one of how it is that the same bad decisions and mistakes are made over and over again in some organisations (Vecchio et al, 1996) and how this can be avoided. Poor decisions made in well-known child protection tragedies from Maria Colwell to Baby Peter Connelly have become notorious. Decisions are made at all levels of social service organisations, and decisions at all levels can be 'bad' decisions. They can be related to an individual tragic case or to a failed broad policy or strategy, for example, Walker (1986) drew attention to the decision in many local authorities to build sheltered housing for older people when the physical needs of those seeking help clearly indicated that something much more akin to high dependency housing was actually required. Vecchio et al's (1996) approach to repeated mistakes is to urge the study of the decision process, and to make sure that decision-making is 'done properly'.

Models of organisational decision making

Planned and unplanned decisions

We should begin by carefully distinguishing the types of decisions we are discussing in this chapter. When we look at the typical decisions of a working day, we find that it is possible to distinguish personal and organisational decisions, planned (or routine) and unplanned decisions. Some examples of these are given in Figure 4.1.

Figure 4.1: Everyday decisions

	Personal	Organisational
Planned	Lunchtime hours Where to park Daily routine	Routine social work decisions
Unplanned	Applying for team leader post	Closure of a residential home
	Specialising in a client group	

Vecchio (2000) observes that there is a constant slippage of unplanned decisions into planned decisions. This might at first sight look like organisations increasingly exercising control, but it is not necessarily so because, unless a system is completely closed, there are always new unplanned contingencies to deal with. Only a closed system, in which all eventualities were known, would allow a fixed distinction between planned and unplanned decisions, therefore, and in practice this is unlikely to include any organisation open to the influences of contemporary society.

Classical model

Herbert Simon (1979) identified two models of decision making in organisations, the classical model and the administrative model. The classical model seems very similar to that presupposed by classical economics: a reasoning individual in the organisation encounters or identifies a choice or a problem, gathers information, and identifies alternative solutions or choices, evaluates these, selects an alternative, implements it, and evaluates its effectiveness. The historical accuracy of this model of economic decision making has been a subject of considerable debate. It is, for example, possible to see economic efficiency as a social construction, rather than as a timeless touchstone or point of reference for economic decision making (Fligstein, 1992). Indeed, there is some evidence that entrepreneurs' decision making in the 'heroic' age of later nineteenth-century business organisations was more about controlling competition than about cheapening goods (Galambos, 1970). That is to say, decisions may not have been governed by considerations of economic efficiency or innovation, but by wider strategies to control markets.

Yet whatever the historical reality of the classical model of decision making in organisations, the reader may perhaps recognise the familiar outline of the social work cycle (Coulshed, 1991) in the decision-making model of classical economics. As with the social work cycle, the reader may recognise a formalised representation of what is in reality a much more fragmented, messy and simultaneous process of overlapping and reiterated stages. However, the formal linear version is arguably the model of social work decision making assumed by the NHS and Community Care Act 1990 insofar as the Act presupposes an unbiased assessor and a client with choice of a range of services.

Administrative model

The administrative model of decision making in organisations, by contrast, is an attempt to describe how decisions are made in practice, rather than theorise how they should or could be made. A key feature of actual decision making behaviour is freedom within limits or bounded discretion. In social work terms, this could be the constraints of a policy or practice framework, or the effect that inevitable resource constraints have in practice upon decision making: there is little gain for the client in being assessed as suitable for a service that the social worker knows is not available.

Decision-making models for social work

Golensky identified no fewer than seven different models of decision making relevant to social work practice. This is an adapted and enlarged version of her list (2011, p 88):

1. Muddling through
2. Garbage can: decisions in search of a problem they fit
3. Vroom-Jago: decide rationally how far to involve others (eg service user)
4. Intuitive: 'I had an uneasy feeling from the outset'
5. Rational: evidence-based info-gathering
6. Decision matrix: maps risks and benefits, can be numerical
7. Pattern recognition: experienced workers look for situational patterns.

Accountability models

Some models of decision making emphasise the discontinuities and dubious individual accountability in some organisational decisions. There is a postmodern model of decision making, described by Jackson and Carter (2000), in which no individual decision making occurs: there is no moment of decision and decisions are distributed. Applying this model, the older case notes now appear to tell the truth: the casework process itself, as a whole, is the decision. In some respects this resembles the pragmatic 'muddling through' and 'garbage can' models described by Golensky (2011). However, Jackson and Carter reject this model and instead opt for a definition of decision making as 'a process informed by the social, political, and economic role of organisations' (2000, p 219). In short, they are arguing that the entire context of the organisation should figure in any analysis of decision making: the budgetary constraints, the political colour of the local authority and the relationship the organisation has with service users and the public as a whole all feed into the decisions.

O'Sullivan (1999) offers a social work model which, while certainly distanced from the absence of individual accountability apparent in the postmodern model, nonetheless accepts that a chain of individual decisions are involved in the social work process. These decisions are made not only by the social worker, but also by the referring person, by the administrative staff, by allocation, by service delivery staff, by relatives and, last but not least, by the service user themselves. O'Sullivan's model adopts the classical model's emphasis upon the systematic evaluation of options, while at the same time encouraging the social worker to take into account emotions and biases. Finally, it advises a critical awareness of organisational context, a maximisation of client involvement and full stakeholder consultation. This reiterates Vecchio et al's (1996) exhortation to be aware of the decision-making process, and to do it properly.

Obstacles to good decision making

Jackson and Carter (2000) have pointed out that, in fact, both the classical and the administrative models assume a rational decision maker and a moment of decision, and also imply detachment of the decision maker from relations of power within the group or in the organisation, detachment from the organisational environment generally and from the unconscious or unexamined preferences or beliefs of the decision maker. That is, both models assume the ability to have an unbiased overview, detachment and emotional restraint, whereas in practice there may be many additional obstacles to effective decision making. For example, the social worker may have a favoured method, such as 'if in doubt, apply for Attendance Allowance', or she may be a newly qualified worker who is worried that she must not be seen to fail, leading her to persist with a bad decision even though events clearly show it to have been wrong, or there may be a 'halo effect' from a particular client placement: 'this home is wonderful, it must be the right placement decision'.

Groupthink

Another obstacle to effective decision making is 'groupthink' (Janis, 1972). This can happen when teams become cosy to the extent that no one wants to rock the boat, and this can effectively constrain individual decision making. Social services committee meetings are often sufficiently politically differentiated to insulate them from this to a large degree, although team meetings, especially meetings of core teams around individual service users, are more likely to succumb to groupthink.

Commitment to a bad decision

Groupthink can also lead to escalation of commitment to a decision despite evidence to the contrary (Festinger, 1962), although this type of escalation can occur in individuals as well as in groups, as noted above in the example of the newly qualified worker not wanting to admit failure. Festinger's study was of a group of UFO watchers and their frustrated expectations of 'rescue' by aliens. When Deliverance Day had come and gone without any sign of intervention by aliens, believers rationalised it with phrases such as 'they are delaying to test us', 'we have not yet prepared their way', and 'we are not yet ready'. This may initially appear to be a far-fetched, off-beat example of decision-making analysis, but there are, arguably, social work parallels. For example, some local authority social services departments persisted with the use of private residential care provision long after the market conditions had ceased to be favourable to purchasers of private care.

Cautious shifts

Risky and cautious shifts (Stoner, 1968) are also obstacles to effective decision making, and can be frequently observed in child protection conferences and elsewhere in client-centred meetings. For example in a cautious shift one person may express serious concerns about the client, perhaps on the basis of behaviour observed only by them, and because everyone else wants to take the safest course of action, they move to the cautious option despite coming to the meeting with a wider range of possible options for the service user. Adult residential placement decisions can also sometimes be prey to the cautious shift.

Individual obstacles

The life experience and background of the social worker can of course also, potentially, affect decisions in an unreasonable or emotional way. For example, consider the occasionally heard phrases 'I had a bad experience with a dog once: don't get involved with clients' pets' and 'Don't make placements out of county, they backfire'.

The media can also influence decision making (Tversky and Kahneman, 1981) and beliefs about whether decisions have been effective. News values, bigotry, stereotypes or, as noted above, public concerns following a child protection tragedy can affect child protection referral figures and decisions made about Child Protection Plans.

Organisational obstacles

What is the role of the organisation in mediating, moderating or circumventing these individual and group obstacles to good decision making, or in facilitating or inhibiting social workers' decisions? O'Sullivan (1999) points out that involving the client, consulting the stakeholders, and management can all be seen as potential obstacles to efficient decision making, despite a general understanding of those things as positive. They can be considered obstacles if we choose to look at them in terms of the delay and complexity they may add to decision making. The impact of client self-determination upon social work decision making was noted as long ago as the 1930s (see Biestek, 1961).

The organisation can also have a moral influence upon the decision maker, and not always positively, perhaps even undermining the rationality of the decision (Ditton, 1977). This could happen when, for example, the decision moves onto legally dubious terrain, or an ethically 'grey area'. A social work example might be the uncertainty in the late 1990s around the role of the 'allowance' accruing to elderly residents of social care homes, under Part III of the National Assistance Act 1948. According to reportage in *Community Care* at that time, there were cases of social worker collusion with residential homes in using the allowance to fund some optional additional services provided by the homes (*Community Care*, 6 June 2000). It was unclear whether this constituted an appropriate discretionary use of the allowance and whether or not local authorities should have covered the cost of all components in the care provided by the home, rather than permitting the allowance to be used for this purpose.

Gender, ethnicity and decision making

As much as any other area of social work practice, decision making calls for those skills of cultural competence and critical reflection that have figured so prominently in social work literature in recent decades. Some additions can be made to O'Sullivan's (1999) otherwise comprehensive model of social work decision making.

In social work, we are dealing with an organisation and its business consisting in large part of the work of women with other women. It is therefore reasonable to ask what effect, if any, gender has upon decision making in the organisation. Iannello (1992) has argued that women attempt to make decisions in a more egalitarian, less hierarchical and more consultative manner than their male counterparts. Examples of this may be found in the empowering organisational forms of women's refuges (Lee, 2001). A difficulty with this decision–making style is that it can appear inefficient, especially in a market environment of the kind that gained ground in social welfare organisations from the 1980s in Britain (Landry, 1985). Landry (1985) indicates that there are obstacles to all team members being involved in every decision, for example information overload (see **Chapter Three**), similar to being deluged with emails which have only slight relevance to the receiver. However, Iannello (1992) maintains that this method can be used in welfare organisations and describes a two–part structure in which all team members communicate and decide on extraordinary matters, while routine, everyday matters are decided by smaller groups. A potential difficulty of managing this is that the relative significance of any particular decision may not be agreed upon by all team members.

Although organisational behaviour textbooks have also become increasingly attuned to an ethnically diverse workforce and customer base, the legacy of organisational behaviour research from earlier periods continues to exert an influence, and this is nowhere more obvious than in the models of decision making reviewed briefly in this chapter. This is not to say that the models are wrong but, rather, that they are often based upon observed middle and senior management practices in North American large corporations of the mid-twentieth century. Even if ethnicity is taken into account, the experience of post-segregationist North America must differ from that in modern–day post-colonial Europe. For example, we need to understand how oppressive behaviours from a former colonial era can be enshrined in the occupational hierarchies of large public sector organisations (Jewkes, 1998). While the earlier models do caution the analyst of organisational decision making to be on the look-out for the operation of stereotypes and biases, this essentially individualising focus of O'Sullivan's model might lead to the overlooking of practices built into the organisation itself.

Yet, as O'Sullivan observed in later work (O'Sullivan, 2010), the tendency of social work organisations to concentrate increasingly upon risk assessment checklists, as aids to decision making, highlights the potential for a 'blame' culture. While they appear to offer reassurance, they are fallible and create the illusion of risk control, rather than recognition of uncertainty (Carson and Bain, 2008). Similarly, there are pitfalls to basing decisions on research ('evidence-based practice'), not least of which is the contextually limited character of much research in the social sciences (O'Sullivan, 2010).

Conclusion

So, do your practice decisions seem to make themselves? The argument of this chapter is that part of the problem at least arises from the way in which the decision process itself is conceived. However, if your practice decisions do seem to make themselves, it may be that the organisation in which you work has other decision process problems, such as an over-reliance upon informal tacit decision making (to which we return in **Chapter Ten**, which looks at issues of power), decision avoidance, or even buck-passing. It is possible that you have imported your decision-making practices with you from a previous work organisation, putting your practice at variance with that of your colleagues. However, if the case records of colleagues appear similar in this respect, there may be a culture of accountability invisibility ('footsteps in the snow'), or accountability avoidance. **Chapter Six** on organisational culture continues the analysis of these organisational behaviours.

> ▶**KEY LEARNING POINTS**
>
> - Individual social work decisions are influenced by their organisation context, and this is especially important in inter-organisational decision making
> - There are a number of potential obstacles to good decision making at individual, group and organisation levels
> - Decision making is prey to influence and bias, both conscious and unconscious, and this has implications for reflective practice
> - Decisions made in the group are influenced by power and status, particularly with regard to gender and ethnicity, and this has implications for service user empowerment

CHAPTER FIVE

Team working: can you join the perfect social work team?

> **What you will learn in this chapter**
> * The differences between teams and groups
> * Theories of teams and team working, including team roles and dynamics
> * Why we have social work teams and what they look like
> * Organisational context for social work teams
> * Impact of multi-professional working on social work teams
> * Importance of gender, sexuality and ethnicity on team working

Introduction

This chapter critically considers team role theories in their application to social work, and looks at the recent evolution of social work teams. We will look at to what extent team working occurs in social work and whether social work teams are like teams in other organisations. We will see that the reality of team working in social work organisations is complex and is not easily mapped by classical theories of teams in the organisational behaviour literature. Possible reasons for this are considered, including the emotional nature of front-line social work, the gendered character of the job, the historical development of social work, resource limitations in social work and recent organisational change.

Why should social workers study team structure?

Many job descriptions of social work posts continue to encourage applicants to reflect upon their potential contributions as a team member. Additionally, area and service delivery units continue to be described as 'teams', and team meetings are usually a standing item in the social services calendar. The National Occupational Standards for social work also emphasise the importance of team working to the social work role.

In the mid-twentieth century, the American sociologist Wilensky (1964) perceptively stated that:

> the occupational group of the future will combine elements from both the professional and bureaucratic models; the average professional man [sic] will combine professional and non-professional orientations; [...]

mixed forms of control, hybrid organisations are the likely outcomes. (Wilensky, 1964, p 57)

This was certainly to prove true of social work as an occupational group: social workers in both the United States and Britain are controlled both by their professional associations and by the organisations in which they work. Because of the strong link to a professional association, training courses devote more and more time to the professional aspects of social work, such that social services complain about social workers' relative lack of preparation 'for the actual job itself'. This raises the question of whether preparing the newly qualified social worker for work in a bureaucracy or quasi-bureaucracy with complex procedures and working conditions is perhaps not adequate to prepare the social worker for practice. As we saw in **Chapter One**, one of the ways in which an organisation influences the practice of social workers is through the structure of the working group. One important question to ask here is therefore: just how does organisational influence through the working group operate?

What makes a team?

Researching the US Army, George (1971) analysed 'buddying', which can be considered the simplest form of team unit. Buddying is a mutual arrangement, perhaps initially set up on the basis of friendship, or it might work the other way around: buddying might lead to a friendship. Either way, the organisational folk-wisdom, based on the sort of mystical loyalty beloved of Hollywood war films, is clear: without a buddy, you'll never make it. George (1971) insisted that, on the contrary, buddying has no mystical qualities, despite the significance sometimes accorded to it in the US Army. Rather it has a simple pragmatic element: your 'buddy' is someone who will stand in for you if necessary, someone who knows what you are doing, someone to help with the occasional practical minutiae of the day's work. For the social worker, this might translate into practical help when you leave your money at home and need petrol, for example, or when you need a lift home when sick, or someone from whom you can get practical advice on day-to-day work. Interestingly, buddying is currently becoming popular as part of induction programmes in some British public sector organisations.

Larger groups, sometimes referred to as primary groups, again do not have to be affiliations of groups of individuals (if we continue the Hollywood war film analogy this would be the close-knit squadron or platoon); they can be made up of a series of two-person relationships. So far, this gives us a very loose idea of a working group, but it does not begin to tell us anything about roles within the group, or about the distribution of skills or the nature of team work. Adair (1986) does not make too much of the distinction between working groups and teams, other than to imply that formally constituted working groups and groups in competition are more likely to be styled as 'teams'.

It should also be pointed out that George's (1971) work is based upon research with men only. Research on women's friendships indicates that they work differently from men's friendships (Coates, 2009), so these concepts may not be applicable.

Indeed, much of the theorisation of team behaviour and roles is based on research with men and this perhaps accounts for an essentially 'football team' approach to human relationships in work groups, in which each individual has a defined and complementary role (Belbin, 1993).

From the point of view of organisational behaviour, the group's task or goal and its culture are likely to be substantially influenced by the organisation as a whole, independently of the roles taken up within the group by its members. Opie (2000) made this point forcibly in her research of interdisciplinary teams in primary care, when she argued that it is not sufficient to assess the functionality or dysfunctionality of teams solely on the basis of the individual psychologies of team members. We should consider the impact of externally imposed power (a radical view) as well as individual dispositions (an interactionist view) and the internal power structure of the group.

Classic theories of teams and team working

Team roles

Benne and Sheats (1948) noted that previous studies tried to identify leader roles and so analysed team member roles. They found three types of member roles, which provide another commonsense typology that could be used in everyday work teams:

1. Task oriented: the people tackling the job
2. Group oriented: the people tackling the group, rather than the job
3. Individual needs oriented: the people tackling neither the task nor the group, looking only to themselves.

There are 27 sub-types in this typology! These are shown in Figure 5.1.

Figure 5.1: Benne and Sheats' subtypes of team member roles

Task-oriented roles	Group-oriented roles	Individual-oriented roles
Initiator–contributor	Encourager	Aggressor
Information seeker	Harmoniser	Blocker
Opinion seeker	Compromiser	Recognition seeker
Information giver	Expediter	Self-confessor
Opinion giver	Standard setter	Playboy
Elaborator	Group observer	Dominator
Coordinator	Follower	Help seeker
Orienter		Special interest pleader
Evaluator–critic		
Energiser		
Procedural technician		
Recorder		

Source: Adapted from Benne and Sheats (1948)

Benne and Sheats (1948) argue that well-trained members take the appropriate role at the right time, avoiding a fixed role. The least effective working group has too many individual-oriented team members (some Social Services Committee meetings come to mind!).

In another major theory of team roles, Belbin (1981) returned to the 'relatively enduring' roles that specific individuals prefer to play in groups. Belbin developed a useful tool for identifying people's preferred team role (as well as your preferred learning style). The team roles, and their strengths and weaknesses, that Belbin (1981) identified were as follows:

- *Plant:* a creative team member, but one who sometimes ignores details.
- *Resource Investigator:* an opportunity explorer, but who tends to be over-optimistic.
- *Co-ordinator* (or *chairperson*): effective at delegation, but can be manipulative.
- *Shaper:* a useful visionary, but can hurt people's feelings.
- *Evaluator:* a standard setter, but who can be overly critical.
- *Teamworker:* a facilitator, but one who can be easily influenced.
- *Implementer:* gets things done, but can be inflexible.
- *Completer:* crosses the ts, but can be irritatingly nit-picking.
- *Specialist:* a knowledgeable team member, but one who can overlook the big picture.

Belbin wanted to construct the perfect team, understanding this to mean a balanced entity with all of the bases covered. A criticism of the theory is that it assumes fixed characteristics ascertained by personality checklists, in which the tests, notoriously, tend to push people into categories. Social constructionists also point to the situation-specific nature of much social behaviour, such that traits do not necessarily endure across time and place.

Figure 5.2: Belbin's team roles

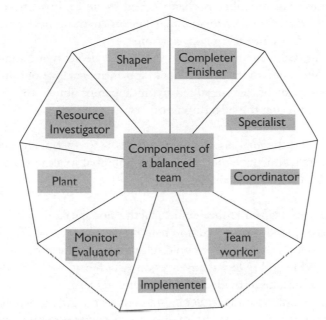

Source: Adapted from Belbin, 1981

Hopefully it will be clear from the above how theories of team roles emerged from scientific attempts to uncover enduring structures of human relationships in groups. Although such theories are open to the obvious criticism that in de-emphasising context they can ignore important organisational influences such as power, culture and organisational purpose, nevertheless this approach to teams remains very popular.

A variant in the study of group processes is that of transactional analysis in organisational working styles. Berne (1963) identified five main working styles arising from psychodynamic compromises established in early childhood, and these five styles comprise a kind of 'team roles' theory. At the risk of over-simplifying a highly sophisticated theory of human behaviour, they are very roughly as follows:

- *Hurry up*: this team member can appear impatient and is always going somewhere more important; she is just too busy to talk to you properly.
- *Be perfect*: with this team member, the simplest job takes forever and is never finished. Verbosity sometimes accompanies this style. This team member is also a poor delegator, can be highly critical of others and does not take criticism very well.

- *Please people*: this team member avoids upsetting people and sometimes gets walked over as a result. She is reluctant to say no and characteristically over-qualifies her opinions, devaluing her own skills and contributions and even her gifts to others.
- *Try hard*: this team member is characterised by an enthusiastic rush at new projects, but rarely finishes them. She takes on anything new, but irritatingly tends to go off at tangents in conversation.
- *Be strong*: this team member displays emotional detachment and a denial of weakness. She seems to strive for a 'mask' and an appearance of calmness under pressure. This can be accompanied by an apparent ability to be unpleasant without considering the effect upon others.

One way of using the analysis of working styles is to encourage individuals to identify their style and, once they know their potential weaknesses, to be able to compensate for them. For example:

- The 'Hurry up' team member could practise not speaking until others have finished talking and learn relaxation techniques.
- The 'Be perfect' team member could tell others that their mistakes are often not irretrievable and reflect themselves on whether it always really matters if they make a mistake (provided things are put right).
- The 'Please people' team member could perhaps try asking people what they want, instead of intuiting it; she might also of course practise saying no and asking others for what she wants to avoid resentment.
- The 'Try hard' team member might make a point of not volunteering for anything and finishing one job before she starts another.
- The 'Be strong' team member could try asking others for help with things even if she thinks she doesn't need it.

Cousins (2010) has made a recent attempt to apply Berne's methods to social work supervision, underlining their continuing relevance.

Team dynamics

The dynamics of the team were not always considered important: before Mayo's studies in the 1920s (Mayo, 1933), a scientific management approach (see **Chapter One**) was considered sufficient to understanding the world of work. From the 1940s attempts were made by several North American psychologists, sociologists and social psychologists to develop a scientific study of groups. This was driven in part by the US military's interest in combat groups, which no doubt led to funding and resources being made available to study group functioning. Rogers (1951), French and Raven (1959), Benne and Sheats (1948) and Bales (1950), among others, developed observational systems for analysing interactions.

Bales: typology of groups

Bales (1950), for example, distinguished twelve types of utterance in meetings within groups:

1. Shows solidarity
2. Shows tension release
3. Shows agreement
4. Gives suggestion
5. Gives opinion
6. Gives information

7. Asks for information
8. Asks for opinion
9. Asks for suggestion
10. Shows disagreement
11. Shows tension
12. Shows antagonism.

As can be seen in the charts from Bales (1950) in Figure 5.3, Bales seems to have envisaged a systematic typology of groups, recognisable by their interaction signatures or profiles. So the group or team, seen as a composite human entity, generated a characteristic algorithm, a collective ethogram. Social work area teams were potentially identifiable by their interaction patterns, and could be distinguished from other types of group. The implication is that deviant group algorithms could be spotted, for example, the dysfunctional or pathological social work team could be identified and the problem diagnosed. A criticism of Bales' approach is that it is reductionist and tells us nothing about the organisational context of the team.

However, Bales' system does offer what seems to be a commonsense approach to team dynamics. The basic approach is to tally the participation of individual team members, which can be followed by an analysis of the type of contribution made. It is the kind of analysis a social worker might find themselves doing during bleak moments in team meetings. Students have used Bales' system while on placement: one student retrospectively analysed a child protection conference through this lens, and another student attempted this with a review meeting. The results were illuminating.

It was only with the popularisation of North American management ideas in Britain after the Second World War, especially from the 1960s onwards, that the study of team dynamics became part of organisational study in Britain.

Figure 5.3: Bales' analysis of meanings

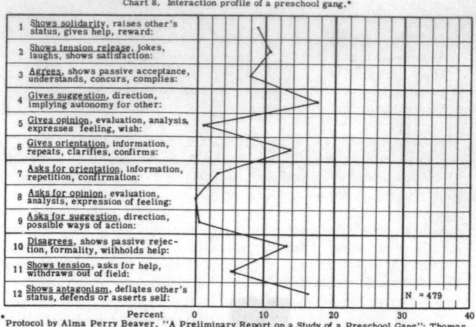

Chart 8. Interaction profile of a preschool gang.*

1	Shows solidarity, raises other's status, gives help, reward:
2	Shows tension release, jokes, laughs, shows satisfaction:
3	Agrees, shows passive acceptance, understands, concurs, complies:
4	Gives suggestion, direction, implying autonomy for other:
5	Gives opinion, evaluation, analysis, expresses feeling, wish:
6	Gives orientation, information, repeats, clarifies, confirms:
7	Asks for orientation, information, repetition, confirmation:
8	Asks for opinion, evaluation, analysis, expression of feeling:
9	Asks for suggestion, direction, possible ways of action:
10	Disagrees, shows passive rejection, formality, withholds help:
11	Shows tension, asks for help, withdraws out of field:
12	Shows antagonism, deflates other's status, defends or asserts self:

N = 479

Percent   0   10   20   30   40

*
Protocol by Alma Perry Beaver, "A Preliminary Report on a Study of a Preschool Gang"; Thomas, Dorothy Swain, and associates, Some New Techniques for Studying Social Behavior, Chap. VI, Bureau of Publications, Teacher's College, Columbia University, New York, N. Y., 1929, 99-117.

Chart 9. Pooled interaction profile for five four-person groups of 9th grade boys.

1	Shows solidarity, raises other's status, gives help, reward:
2	Shows tension release, jokes, laughs, shows satisfaction:
3	Agrees, shows passive acceptance, understands, concurs, complies:
4	Gives suggestion, direction, implying autonomy for other:
5	Gives opinion, evaluation, analysis, expresses feeling, wish:
6	Gives orientation, information, repeats, clarifies, confirms:
7	Asks for orientation, information, repetition, confirmation:
8	Asks for opinion, evaluation, analysis, expression of feeling:
9	Asks for suggestion, direction, possible ways of action:
10	Disagrees, shows passive rejection, formality, withholds help:
11	Shows tension, asks for help, withdraws out of field:
12	Shows antagonism, deflates other's status, defends or asserts self:

N = 1870

Percent   0   10   20   30   40

Source: Bales, 1950, p 23.

Practice example: team dynamics – norming, storming and forming

Lucy Makwedze joined a children with disabilities team after qualifying, where she settled in gradually over her probationary period. She had a disabled child herself and, as well as her expertise around developmental aspects of the disability, she found a place in the team as someone who was especially skilled at working with parents who were struggling to cope.

The metropolitan social services department in which Lucy worked underwent reorganisation. As a consequence of this her team was merged with another, creating one team covering the whole of the north side of the city, and moved to a well-adapted modern building, sharing administrative support.

Lucy found that the team with which hers had merged had been very recently reconstituted, as most of the members had reached retirement age simultaneously and had been replaced by new workers. They were clearly still getting to know one another, as Lucy had difficulty finding out some colleagues' names. In team meetings, workers clustered into pairs in the large, well-lit, new meeting room, and the team leader's notices were followed by sharp assertions by individual members about working practices in their previous teams. These were interspersed by long silences. At lunchtimes people just seemed to disappear. Although Lucy's former colleagues still came to her for advice and to engage her help with some cases, her new colleagues did not discuss cases with her. To make matters worse, the cases she was allocated seemed not to acknowledge her expertise.

At lunch with a member of the old team one day, Lucy reflected that since the merger everything seemed chaotic. Her colleague agreed and hinted that she was looking for another job, with a 'more settled' team.

Buchanan and Huczynski (2004) start from the assumption that, when in a group, we individually behave in predictable ways, regardless of whether the group is formal (such as a football team) or informal (for example, a walking group), and regardless of the appointed task of the group.

Bales (1950) took the view that the sum of the group members' roles creates equilibrium. If there is no equilibrium, the group collapses, or changes until there is. He seems to have been less interested in groups with permanent conflict. This is also incidentally the functionalist theory of the family developed by Parsons (Parsons, 1951; Parsons and Shils, 1951), a colleague of Bales.

Furthermore, the method of Randall and Southgate (1980), briefly referred to elsewhere in this chapter, is also a psychodynamic approach to team dynamics, and like that of Berne, has its origins in the work of Freud. Unlike Berne's approach, however, it follows Wilhelm Reich in viewing team activity as a cyclical, energy-building and energy-releasing process. Such approaches tend to focus attention away from the organisational context of teams, however.

Finally, French and Raven (1959) distinguished five types of power in groups: reward power, coercive power, referent power (desirable traits that should be copied), legitimate power (authority), and expert power (superior knowledge).

What do social work teams look like?

Why are social work teams necessary? The core task of much social work is still casework, and the casework relationship is an individual one (Biestek, 1961), so why are teams important, except insofar as they consist of loose aggregates of case-working individuals? The 'teams' of individual case-holding social workers of the 1970s described by Payne (1982) arguably do have some of the characteristics of groups rather than teams, insofar as there is limited specialisation or complementarity of roles described by Belbin (1993). While the self-managing, networking teams of the 1990s (Payne, 2000) may have role specialisation, they do not necessarily have the team interdependence described by Belbin's approach (1993).

In his research on social work teams, Payne (1982) distinguished teams from work groups. An area team, understood simply as a work group, would consist of the number of workers required to cover the cases within the geographical area covered by the team. However, Payne argued that area teams are more than that: as a collaborative group, the team takes account of the specific skills and personal development needs of team members. So, for example, allocation is not just a simple one-for-you, one-for-me dividing up of the incoming work, but a collaborative event in which team members cooperate to deal with particular pressures in ways that take account of individual skills and personal development. This does not mean that a workload management scheme cannot be operated simultaneously by a manager, incidentally.

However, where team leaders are appointed, this may undermine the self-managing interdependence of team members upon one another. In short, organisational structure and leadership and management both have a significant effect upon team dynamics, and upon each other.

Payne (1982) also noted two broad theoretical approaches to team dynamics:

1. A working group moves, more or less, along a continuum between work group and collaborative group, largely as a function of internal dynamics.
2. The dynamic of the team is mainly a function of its organisational position and function.

Reflective point: Consider how both these theories of group dynamics can be used to understand your own social work team, or other teams in which you have worked

Using the second of these approaches we could compare, say, a residential team and a team of middle managers. Although there may be some similarities in team dynamics, the tasks, objectives and working conditions will clearly be a major determinant of who is interacting with whom and to what purpose; residential workers on the same shift, for example, might form an important subgroup. Also, when taking this view it can be seen that a team in which casework is highly individual is not necessarily ineffective as a team but simply meeting organisational requirements. How individual team members experience such a team is of course another matter.

Skills and roles in social work teams

Overall, Payne (1982) reinforces Timms' (1970) observation that the different organisational settings of social work teams – penal system, education, hospital, residential and community settings for example – have a major influence on the social worker's relationships with colleagues within their teams and with clients. Writing prior to the creation of local authority social services departments that followed the Local Authority Social Services Act 1970, Timms (1970) was however aware of the generic model of social work training waiting in the wings, and he questioned quite how this would square with the then-existing specialisms. Stevenson (1980) subsequently looked back on this and noted how those who anticipated the generic model of individual practice in the 1971 reorganisation were 'blown off course almost at once'(Stevenson, 1980, p 14) by a combination of workforce conservatism and the need to have specialist skills and experience in prioritised work. Stevenson's research found that the structure of teams following the 1970s reorganisation of social services often appeared unchanged from the structure of teams before the reorganisation in certain respects. For example, social work assistants were no one's assistant in the teams before reorganisation and, in many teams, continued to perform similar work to that of qualified workers afterwards. In particular, children and families continued to receive prioritisation within teams despite a supposedly generic approach, showing that organisational priorities continued to constrain the work that teams and their members actually undertook. Individual casework remained the dominant model, with shared working being rare (Payne, 1982) and social work assistants not being assigned lesser parts of shared cases, as was perhaps envisaged by the policy makers. This 'privatised' style of working within teams was also encouraged by the 'patch' working system (Hadley and Hatch, 1981) in which social workers took responsibility for a particular geographical area, a system which received an additional fillip with nominal attachment to general medical surgeries in some local authorities towards the millennium and after.

It is interesting that team caseloads on the American model seem not to have been formally considered (Briggs, 1980), and that the construction of heterogeneous teams of specialists was either deemed unfeasible or undesirable.

Since the 1970s there has been informal specialisation within teams (although Stevenson, 1980, notes that community workers were formally created during this period and typically formed separate teams), although this is perhaps increasingly being overcome by tendencies towards homogenisation of tasks inherent in processes such as that of care management (Dustin, 2007). Specialisation survived nevertheless in the life-stage division of teams into adults and children and families respectively, which accelerated following the Children Act 1989 and the NHS and Community Care Act 1990. The development of separate intake and long-term teams, which began at least as early as the 1970s, is also an example of a formal specialisation model of social work teams operating with the informal specialisation model. The process of allocation by case rather than role has tended to resist the individual development of formal specialism within teams, even within life-stage teams. In some teams social workers do not want to give up a particular area of work to one 'specialist' worker.

Organisational context for social work teams

Another development in team working during the 1970s was the attempt to fuse community work with casework in some area teams, leading to unitary teams in which group supervision and other forms of group-working could also operate (Holder and Wardle, 1981). This was an important move within the voluntary sector in the late 1970s. This model collapsed in the 1980s, partly because of the acknowledged difficulty of measuring outcomes or performance and because some forms of collective team performance, of agency decision making and tasks for example, were seen to be inefficient (Randall and Southgate, 1980; Landry, 1985). The political removal of community workers from public funding in the mid-1980s may also have been a factor in their demise. Attempts to keep community social work going in area teams through training (Smale and Tucson, 1988) were confronted by the harsh realities of budgetary constraints and the prioritisation of statutory obligations during the 1990s. More recently, however, community development work has emerged within Health Trusts, and social work training and liaison with community work has continued for a period.

The new public management approach that swept into social services during the 1980s and 1990s (see **Chapter Eight**) brought with it a renewed emphasis upon managerial approaches to the team, taken from business management literature. In his book on team work, Payne (2000) acknowledged the effect that the move to compulsory competitive tendering, the purchaser–provider split, partnership working with service users and inter-professional working had made upon social work in teams. Social work teams of the 1970s were essentially part of a rational–bureaucratic organisation structure, multi-layered, hierarchical and relatively compartmentalised, with little influence upon or communication with one another. Inter-agency working required new forms, and 'matrix structure' teams, with members drawn from different levels and areas of the (bureaucratic) organisation, were one response to this. However, these types of teams suffered from problems of their own, such as the tendency to preserve the hierarchical and accompanying power relations of the parent organisation.

Another new type of team dynamic facilitated by the changed organisational structure of new managerialism was the open or outward-looking team, needed partly to fulfil the growing requirement to engage in partnership with service users (Beresford and Croft, 1990) and because of the inter-organisational working increasingly demanded by care management, child protection, carer and other legislation (Jelphs and Dickinson, 2008). As West (2004) and others have pointed out, however, open team working will fail within a traditional, hierarchically structured organisation with impermeable divisional boundaries; to succeed the organisation needs to be structured around the teams.

Multi-professional social work teams

Webster (2010) and Hammick et al (2009) have drawn attention to specific issues in multi-professional team working. There are a number of potential obstacles to the effective functioning of multi- and inter-professional teams. For example, confidentiality protocols in different organisations may appear to be of little concern until professionals from different organisations need to share information regarding a service user. Differential organisational cultures and power levels can also cause difficulties, although this is not discussed in the literature.

At the interpersonal level within multi-professional teams, Webster (2010) suggests using a dialogical approach coupled to a storytelling method as a way of exploring and sharing the varied roles of team members. A technique for training days is to construct a team 'story', with the accounts laid out on paper consecutively to capture and share the interpersonal reality of the team as a whole.

A common occurrence with multi-professional working is the assembly of a large group of team members at the home of a service user, which can be intimidating for the service user but at least allows everyone to see the barrage of professionals individually visiting the service user, who would otherwise often be unbeknown to one another. Another issue is that of the unplanned professional encounter. Imagine, for example, an adult mental health professional arriving at the home of a service user to meet with a psychiatrist to jointly assess and decide upon a course of action. Without prior discussion, the meeting can be an awkward and even ill-prepared professional encounter for all parties. Sometimes there is no alternative, although some workers will practise networking (or 'nobbling', as it is often, although incorrectly, described), contacting their inter-agency colleagues before or after the meeting to ensure smooth proceedings.

Payne's (2000) work coincides to an extent with that of Opie (2000) on multidisciplinary teams in primary care. Like Payne, Opie sees the client as being, in a sense, part of the team. Opie, however, takes a postmodern, discourse–analytical and Foucauldian perspective, in which the team performs knowledge work within which representations of the client and family are produced by the intersection of discrete professional discourses. The intersection of these discourses (and the inclusion, exclusion or marginality of knowledges within these discourses) is a product of the operation of power within and between discourses.

Applying the classical theories to social work teams

In Britain the management focus on teams in social services shifted from the 1980s towards using team dynamics to empower local self-management as layers of management were stripped out of public services in attempts at de-bureaucratisation. Also, teams were trained in total quality management (see **Chapter Nine**), with its emphasis upon team self-monitoring and a culture of continuous self-improvement with the team driving improvements to services. One immediate impact of these changes in the use of teams was that fortnightly team meetings tended to become management briefing sessions, with two or even three hours sometimes consumed with management notices about new expectations, policies and procedures. 'Networking' became a team buzzword as teams were opened up by the assignment of team members to liaise with various external agencies (Payne, 2000).

Interestingly, colleagues in some social services area teams apply this concept of the networked team in a slightly different way. To them, the designated 'core group' of professionals from various agencies working around a particular service user most resembles the interdisciplinary networked team, while the area 'team' to which they belong resembles a 'group' insofar as it consists of relatively autonomous individual case-holders. One lesson to be learned from this may be that attempts to distinguish groups from teams in any conclusive way are not helpful in the study of social work organisations. An alternative inference may be that the definition of teams in terms of specialist contributory skills, or in terms of the power base of team members, may simply reflect the outlook of male organisational members upon which much of the research into teams has in the past been based, as has been noted previously. Iannello (1992) and others have suggested that women do not typically teamwork in this way when left to organise themselves, such as in women's refuges. This might then help to explain why some of the classical literature on team roles sometimes seems an uneasy fit with experiences in social work organisations.

In the late 1990s 'hot-desking' became a popular workplace arrangement in social services, but this had an impact on teams: Millward et al (2007) found that hot-desking weakened team identification but strengthened organisational identification. Similarly, there was a renewed management focus upon diversity in teams in social services. Bezrukova et al (2009) found that demographic splits in teams, such as those of age, tended to correlate with perceived poorer performance. However, this could be counterbalanced in some ways by team identification, and strategies for increasing team self-identification, such as the naming of work teams in social services and their competition on targets, were attempted in some local authorities.

Wageman and Gordon (2005) found that, perhaps unsurprisingly, the values of individuals affected their group performance. Those individuals with democratic values working with similar others showed high interdependence, whereas those with meritocratic values showed low interdependence. Interestingly, mixed groups were the worst-performing groups.

Bechky (2006) studied temporary teams and found that, contrary to the stereotype of instability, such groups used enthusiastic thanking, polite admonition and role-oriented joking to learn and negotiate role structures. This can be applied to client-centred multidisciplinary team working.

Gender, sexuality, ethnicity and team working

In an interesting historical sidelight on the development of social work teams, Hall and Hall (1980) describe research in the mid-1970s in which team working was specifically used to address the substantial numbers of part-time social workers in some local authority social services departments. Although they noted that employers preferred to employ full-time social workers they could not always get them, so, given the tendency of family care responsibilities to fall upon women and the preponderance of women in the social work workforce, some found themselves employing substantial numbers of part-time social workers (as high as 38.9% of the social work workforce in one London borough in 1975). Hall and Hall (1980) found little to object to in team arrangements for the organisational management of a part-time social workforce, and it is tempting to believe that this had significance for the development of teams in social work especially in the light of equal opportunities legislation from the 1970s onwards.

Korczynski (2003) researched front-line service workers and found that teams operated as communities of coping, performing collective emotional labour. In the literature on social work teams, this function of teams is often referred to as 'useful support'; however, Korczynski sees this as a skilled team activity (see also Payne, 2000). Korczynski argues that front-line service workers are usually women and suggests that this is because women possess greater skills for dealing with the disappointment, frustration and anger which sometimes occur when the rational logic of production and retail occasionally 'shows through' the performance of customer sovereignty. He also found that air hostesses and call centre operatives recognised behavioural indicators and absorbed one another's feelings of humiliation, hurt, frustration and shock.

Dressel (1987) argues that workplace teams are the means whereby men control and regulate the emotional labour of women in front-line social work. The managed team is where the official version of the task is imposed upon the messy business of confronting human suffering: team meetings, individual supervision and administrative process frame behaviour at the interface between social services and the client in what Opie (2000) has called the discourses of power and control.

Hearn and Parkin (2001) maintain that organisations have an implicit sexuality structured into them, so it is interesting to ask if this may be true also of team roles. They studied teams of residential social workers and concluded that gay workers were sometimes deselected from certain sorts of work, such as escort work with vulnerable same-sex clients. Although interesting, the evidence used by Hearn and Parkin (2001) was insufficient to support a generalisable conclusion.

The ethnic or cultural composition of teams, and for that matter of organisations and service users, should be revisited in the context of our overview of the organisational behaviour literature on teams. Social workers belonging to minority ethnic groups may find that, in terms of the typologies of team roles examined, they are relegated to the role of 'expert' based on their perceived culture or ethnic background, or country of origin of their ancestors, regardless of their other strengths or contributions to the team.

Conclusion

Teams are perhaps rather like good neighbours: if you find a good team, nurture it; if the members move, move with them! Diagnosing what is wrong in an area team that has become notorious in a local authority for one reason or another is possible using the theories discussed in this chapter, and then it is sometimes possible to put things right. Although social work teams are still in many ways groups of individual caseworkers, there are nevertheless team functions, and buddying is, arguably, indispensable. A divided team will affect even the most determined individual caseworker sooner or later, if only by obstructing information flows. It will also certainly make a negative impression upon service users, as well as perhaps affecting decision making, motivation, supervision and other aspects of organisational behaviour. Becoming aware of team dynamics and behaving accordingly is an organisational skill that can be developed like any other, so we should perhaps aim to get more out of team meetings, look forward to training days and accept nominations to task groups willingly (if cautiously).

We have seen that in the traditional organisational behaviour literature teams have been defined to a considerable extent by the methods used to study them. The literature also tends to be dominated by the idea that team working is intrinsically a good thing. Nevertheless we have seen that, when particular organisations such as the army or social services are examined, the objectives of the organisation can result in teams in which a considerable degree of worker autonomy occurs. If we still wish to use the term 'team' as the unit of analysis of organisational behaviour in social services organisations, we may have to speak of 'open teams' consisting of caseworkers consulting with service users and carers, and liaising with other professional workers in a wide range of partner organisations, rather than seeing teams as tightly knit working groups looking inwards to the organisation and its business. Additionally, we may need to acknowledge that the area team is the focus of diverse discourses into which the service user is inserted by the operation of state power, and that the team is where social workers fit the raw emotional labour of their work into the written records, procedures and policies of the organisation.

There does not appear to be a weight of evidence yet for the complete takeover of self-managing teams (Peters, 1987) in social work organisations, although budget-handling second-tier managers with a broader span of control have, in some local authority social services departments, replaced team leaders. Some team leader functions have then devolved to senior practitioners. If this arrangement results in what can be considered a self-managing team made up of self-managing social workers, the question becomes: how can these teams push forward quality and service user involvement still further?

▶KEY LEARNING POINTS

- The organisational behaviour literature tends to emphasise individual characteristics of group members over the organisational context of the team
- Social work teams are often working groups rather than teams
- Area and life-stage organisation of teams has been the norm in social work, but this is now being modified by interdisciplinary, inter-organisational outward-looking teams involving service users. These multi-professional teams call for specific strategies
- The status of unqualified social workers in teams continues to be ambiguous

▶SEMINAR ORIENTATION: CAN YOU JOIN THE PERFECT SOCIAL WORK TEAM?

Reading: Handy (1993), Chapter 6, or Buchanan and Huczynski (2004), Chapter 12; Lambley (2009), Chapter 6.

▶EXERCISE: TEAM ROLES

What is your preferred team role? What is your 'back-up' role? Complete Belbin's (1993) team roles questionnaire and find out. Compare your findings with those of other students. Are there typical team roles that social workers tend to prefer, and, if so, what are they?

CHAPTER SIX

Organisational culture: do social services have a culture of complaint or a culture of care?

What you will learn in this chapter
- Development of organisational culture as a concept
- The roles of organisational subcultures
- Approaches to organisational change
- The impact of service user involvement on social work organisational culture
- Gendered aspects of organisational cultures
- Impact of organisational cultures on individual identity

Introduction

This chapter examines social work organisations as entities with distinct and identifiable cultures, and links an awareness of this to the mainstream concept of organisational culture in the organisational behaviour literature.

Care organisations can be viewed as little societies having identifiable cultures of their own (Hyde and Davies, 2004). There is a long-standing and well-documented theory that women's sense of responsibility for the care of others essentially creates the characteristic culture of such organisations (O'Brien, 1989; Aronson, 1992; Bowden, 1997; Williams, 2001). Conversely, the 'culture of complaint' (Hughes, 1994) referred to in the title of this chapter suggests an emerging society of service users who are increasingly willing to complain, equipped with rights but lacking similar counterbalancing responsibilities towards others, supported by a culture of 'political correctness' and perhaps blame-avoidance in public services (Hughes, 1994). While acknowledging the divergent theories of the causes and treatment of such behaviour, this chapter will not provide an answer to the question in its title, but will explore something of what the culture of social work organisations might be.

According to Schein (1985), an organisation's culture may originate from the beliefs and values of the founder (for example Barnardo's, The Salvation Army, Alcoholics Anonymous), surrounding societal norms (for example the Distressed Gentlefolk's Society), problems of external integration (for example, a tight charitable funding environment leading to the adoption of a particular identity), or problems of internal integration (for example, differences between social workers and care workers, accentuating differences between the cultures of service units).

Although there are several definitions of organisational culture (Thompson et al, 1996), the understanding used in this chapter is that culture consists of deeply held organisational beliefs about success (Deal and Kennedy, 1999). Notwithstanding the male-competitive tone of this definition, it can be argued that shared conceptions of how the business of the organisation can be successfully negotiated lie at the root of the culture of an organisation. This is so even if success is conceived as simply avoiding catastrophe or even watching one's back.

But why should social workers study organisational culture? Organisational culture can affect individual social work decisions and service quality (O'Sullivan, 1999); it can facilitate or impede accountability in social work (Slater, 1995); it can strengthen or undermine individual morality; it can influence the relationship with the service user, and can impede organisational change designed to improve this (Hyde and Davies, 2004). It can also disempower the social worker, leading to stress and apathy (Thompson et al, 1996); it can be insidious but, arguably, it can be changed (Coulshed et al, 2006). There are also reasons for thinking that organisational culture may be a useful concept in analysing voluntary sector organisations (Harvey, 1980). Finally, organisational culture is sometimes cited in reports of inquiries into disasters in or caused by an organisation, including those in social work. Consider for example the reference to a culture of ignoring safety procedures in the report following the 2010 Gulf of Mexico oil spill, or the reference to a bonus culture and a culture of short-termism in the finance industry following the 2009 financial crash.

We will begin this chapter by considering the specific training culture of social work courses and of the organisational behaviour writing on organisational induction. The history, diversity and potential of the culture of social service organisations will be briefly examined and its potential assessed. The chapter also examines the link between individual identity and organisational culture in practice settings, the oppressive and empowering aspects of organisational culture and the link between organisational change and culture. Social workers will probably recognise at least some of the organisational behaviour debate here, most notably that around subcultures, as connecting with the social work literature on community development. Finally, the prospects for change within social work organisational cultures are considered.

History of organisational cultures

The classic organisational behaviour textbooks of the 1930s and 1940s (such as Simon, 1945; Barnard, 1948) do not include the study of organisational culture. The appearance of organisational culture appears to have followed the rise of Japanese competition in the post-war period (Dawson, 1996). There was a, perhaps naïve, belief that the success of Japanese manufacturers of motorcycles, cars and audio equipment could be replicated by changes in the organisational culture of Western companies. This led to a focus upon attitudes and values in organisations in the 1960s and 1970s, and an understanding of national differences in organisational cultures (see for example Robbins, 1993). In the 1970s, typologies of organisational cultures emerged (for example, Harrison, 1972; Handy,1978), although these linked organisational culture closely to organisational structure, such that public sector bureaucracies unsurprisingly have a typically 'role-oriented' culture, while autocratic private firms have a 'power' culture and service businesses often have a 'task' culture.

By the 1980s organisational culture became a standard element of organisational behaviour, to the extent that it became conventional to discuss dysfunctional cultures and culture change in great detail. Deal and Kennedy (1982), Peters and Waterman (1982) and other writers on business management argued that the most successful businesses of the previous decade had been ones with clearly identifiable organisational cultures that engaged with employee and customer beliefs. This supported a trend for corporate visions and mission statements (it is interesting to discover how many voluntary sector and public sector logos and mission statements were coined or revisited in the 1980s and 1990s).

This also marked a move away from the sometimes anthropological flavour of writing on organisational culture of a decade earlier (a good example of which is Page, *The Company Savage* [1972]), which contributed to the language, methods and theories of organisational behaviour in the 1970s.

Diversity and change in organisational cultures

Organisational analysts in the US were perhaps ambivalent about the value of organisational culture comparisons. Robbins (1993) for example, argued that the Japanese were pragmatists above all else and therefore not bound by cultural emphasis upon loyalty or teamwork; it was a mistake to assume the complete uncritical acceptance of a putative national culture by all the members of a society. This is worth bearing in mind when thinking about the alleged 'resistance' of organisational cultures to change.

Yet, just as it was manufacturing's adoption of 'Japanisation' (such as just-in-time production methods, short production runs and low stock levels) rather than Japanese culture that produced actual change, so it was the restructuring of social services rather than change in organisational culture that brought change to social workers. The first time many social workers heard the phrase 'culture change' was prior to the marketisation of areas of social services in the early 1990s. As it had done earlier in industry, the phrase heralded sweeping reorganisation, and it is tempting to see 'culture change' as a relatively unthreatening way of introducing major structural change in organisations.

Organisational subcultures

We have defined organisational culture as 'deeply held beliefs about success', rather than, say, 'the way we do things around here', or 'the values and norms of the organisation'. Deeply held beliefs about success touch our dreams, fantasies and aspirations about our achievements, our customers' or clients' achievements, and the achievements of the organisation within which we work. Needless to say, the relationship between organisational culture and these dreams and aspirations can be an inverse one, with organisational culture serving to protect the individual from challenge to deeply-held beliefs. For example, the subculture of a service unit can be one of disengagement from the wider organisation.

As an illustration of this, Jermier et al (1991) mapped the subcultures of five clusters of officers in a US police department. They identified several different subcultures of resistance to the 'official' culture of their organisation, including 'ass-covering legalists', 'peace-keeping moral entrepreneurs', 'anti-military social workers', and 'crime-fighting street professional'. The only subculture they could find that was closely aligned with the official culture of crime-fighting command bureaucracy was that of 'crime-fighting commandos'. It is not difficult to see how versions of the subcultures identified by Jermier et al (1991), for example 'peace-keeping moral entrepreneurs' or 'ass-covering legalists' could be identified in some area social work teams confronting an 'official' (in Jermier et al's terms) organisational culture of best value or compulsory competitive tendering. Such subcultures might protect deeply held beliefs about the vocational, non-marketisable nature of care for others (Harris, 2003). However, not all subcultures are positive.

For example, some 'heroic' unit cultures, in which a particular unit manager is lionised, can be autocratic and not very participative (O'Sullivan, 1999). Subcultures can also embody opposition and resentment towards other groups of workers perceived to be better off, resulting in non-cooperation, blaming, point-scoring and, because of poor liaison, a potentially poorer service to customers (Davis, 1985).

The induction of new employees into existing subcultures

Vecchio (2000) refers to the shared norms and values taught to new employees as introduction to the organisational culture. In an area social services office, these may not necessarily coincide exactly with professional social work ethics or expressed local government policy. For example, the new employee may encounter routine practices of working unpaid overtime, missing lunch, organising 'socials' and doing extramural voluntary work; or they may encounter cynicism, 'us and them' ways of referring to service users, mutual care between social workers and parochialism. Methods of informal induction into the organisational culture typically include the telling of organisational myths and stories (Vecchio, 2000), and these can certainly be found in social services settings. Here are some examples from practice and placement settings:

"There's a chap in Finance who uses a map and ruler on mileage claims" (while inducting a new social worker into arrangements for claiming mileage expenses).

"That manager over there comes in on Saturdays and goes through desk drawers…. One social worker hid all his difficult case files at the back of a drawer" (while explaining the arrangements for case recording and confidentiality).

"There was a university lass started here who wrote a court report so bad they sent it back" (during induction into record-keeping). (The reader may also detect a cultural devaluation of classroom learning.)

These are all good examples of induction into a 'watch your back' organisational culture.

Organisational subcultures seem to be less important to staff retention than the congruity in values between social worker and supervisor (Wu and Hu, 2009). However, the impact of organisational culture upon performance is notoriously difficult to measure and, as organisational behaviour writers say, 'what can't be measured, can't be managed' (Deal and Kennedy, 1999). Even so, the impact of subcultures in social services should not be underestimated. It is possible to see the enduring problems of some service units in sub-cultural terms – an approach that will resonate with social workers with a youth work background in particular. Just as British youth and community workers were encouraged in the 1970s to identify the core aspirational elements of sometimes baffling subcultures, in the 1990s managers were being urged to identify surviving subcultures in downsized, merged and restructured business organisations (Deal and Kennedy, 1999). It was recognised that such subcultures not only kept people going in their jobs, but also continued to exact high levels of service and commitment from employees. Given the positive potential of these subcultures, if managers could somehow link them to a revitalised organisational vision, a competitive advantage might be obtained.

Similar thinking to this can be seen in attempts to ensure continuing high levels of service to clients in the wake of the purchaser–provider split in social services in the 1990s. It was recognised that many residential, community support and area teams had their own internal loyalties and work cultures, together with low levels of absenteeism and often considerable involvement in work beyond their job roles. These subcultures had survived restructuring, and offered potential models for repairing some of the demoralising divisions within social services. For example, the subcultures of some residential units were seen as old-fashioned and paternalistic, and little time was lost in restructuring them along compulsory competitive tendering and market lines. But following their restructure, some managers effectively used well-known community work methods to salvage organisational culture: clarified service objectives were conveyed to units, often after celebrating a unit's achievements and retirement parties were used to celebrate the heroes, landmarks and reputation of service units, while at the same time 'rubbing off' the goodwill generated in this way onto the rebranded parent social service organisation, usually with the aid of newsletters or even press coverage (Deal and Kennedy, 1999).

All of this may sound familiar and in line with the current practice in the business sector. Indeed, pulling the social care sector together behind re-iterated common values (HM Government, 2010a) can be seen as a sound business move, restoring customer confidence and employee morale.

Thompson et al (1996) studied and compared social workers' stress levels in three area offices before looking for aspects of the organisation that might account for the particularly high levels of stress found in one of the offices. At the risk of distorting a complex and careful study their findings might be very briefly summarised as follows. In the office with the highest stress levels the social workers appeared to be going through the motions of the job without any real sense of control; they were procedural rather than committed, and had a despairing sense of unacknowledged difficulties, implying organisational indifference. The researchers postulated a negative, destructive subculture of pessimism to explain the higher stress levels, based on the assumption that doubts about efficacy, feelings of pointlessness and invisibility undermine positive and constructive initiatives before they get off the ground.

Changing organisational cultures

The extent to which it is possible to change the culture of an organisation is disputable (Thompson et al, 1996), although there have been several attempts to outline ways of doing so. Vecchio et al (1996) identified the following approaches to changing an organisation's culture:

* altering what managers measure and control;
* changing crisis response;
* altering induction;
* mentoring;
* altering rewards;
* changing hiring and promotion.

In social work these could be connected to compulsory competitive tendering, changes to weekend working, value matching at interview, ending long service leave and implementing accelerated progression.

From Thompson et al's (1996) study of workplace stress in social work, the culture change measures suggested were very similar to those later identified by Deal and Kennedy (1999). These measures are:

* identifying the subculture;
* consulting with staff to construct a vision and mission statement;
* acknowledging and rewarding effort;

- implementing supervision that reinforced shared values; and
- maintaining empowerment through the use of the team as a group.

A particular advantage of this approach is the recognition that organisational cultures are not one-dimensional; that they can and usually do contain divisions (subcultures), conflict and grey areas. It is a noted weakness of mainstream business approaches to organisational culture that they tend to be functionalist and to overlook flux and ambivalence (Jackson and Carter, 2000). Acknowledging a negative subculture within an organisation is a particularly difficult part of changing organisational culture, as anyone who has experienced this will know. Staff may experience this 'outing' of their workplace as yet more evidence of their impotence and of the organisation's misunderstanding and devaluing of their efforts. In short, being told that a workplace has a 'bad' culture which needs changing provides yet more evidence (if more were needed) of the parent organisation's determination to devalue it.

A further weakness of the 'subcultural rebuild' approach lies in its potentially uncritical acceptance of surviving service unit subcultures which may not be positive. No matter how many copies of the Code of Practice (GSCC, 2002) are distributed, team-building away-days arranged or metaphorical group hugs given, a paranoid subculture with a history of grievance procedures and a generalised attitude of suspicion, defensiveness and fear, is likely to remain paranoid because this has been a successful survival strategy (Deal and Kennedy, 1999; O'Sullivan 1999).

Brown (1998) examined five different models of organisational culture change, with objectives ranging from changing 'over-cautious' cultures with rigid and slow decision making to cultures of individual responsibility, to breaking a traditional culture of restricted management–labour relations to create a culture of customer-focused co-working. Methods used included renaming jobs, service units and departments, changing logos, signage and letterheads; replacing older staff with younger staff, and changing leaders ('cultural elites'); changing the language used by staff to address one another and customers; changing dress codes; holding more frequent staff meetings; circulating newsletters; engaging service users; employing consultants; staging road shows; posting three-year plans; instigating open-door management; and changing the physical appearance of buildings, both inside and out. Although in some of the case studies examined by Brown (1998) there was clear evidence of change to organisational culture, in some it was difficult to tell if organisational culture change had indeed occurred and it was described as being 'in progress'.

Trice and Beyer (1991) have pointed to the significant role of the manager in determining or changing the culture of an organisation or organisational unit, although the existence of subcultures, as discussed above, suggests that senior managers do not necessarily control the cultural dimensions of an organisation.

Service user involvement

As Coulshed et al (2006) pointed out, 'culture change' in social services in the 1980s also heralded major moves towards greater service-user involvement and consultation (see, for example, Beresford, 1980; Beresford and Croft, 1990). Although service user consultation in social work has a history which goes back further than this, the impetus given by management ideas in the 1980s had a major impact in putting it on the agenda. Related to this, the British lecture tour of the American management guru Tom Peters in the early 1980s no doubt popularised his ideas and his book *In search of excellence* (Peters and Waterman, 1982) found its way into Certificate in Management Studies and Diploma in Management Studies curricula for aspiring social services managers at that time. The Quality Protects agenda, in the 1990s reorganisation of children's services following the Children Act 1989, can be seen as an echo of this.

It is interesting to note that the 'service user perspectives' focus in social services in 1990s Britain (as predicted by Simon et al, 1950, almost half a century earlier), was facilitated by the alignment of the existing public sector value of service to others and the social work value of helping others to structural change towards greater service user involvement. In Peters' (1987) reformulation of customer focus in the organisational behaviour literature of the 1980s, he was explicit about the potential value of customer service in the public sector. Peters had been involved in public programmes early in his career and emphasised the value of employee empowerment, cutting bureaucracy and improving service quality in the public sector (Peters, 1987). There is some persistence and recycling of ideas in organisational behaviour, just as there is in social work.

There is a view that resistance to full service-user involvement in public service organisations continues and is partly caused by cultural intransigence (Hyde and Davies, 2004, for example). Examining mental health acute care and hostel support, Hyde and Davies (2004) argue that service user involvement is still similar in certain core respects to that of the institutional care of the 1960s and 1970s, despite recent attempts to change it. They draw upon the work of Melanie Klein to suggest that at the core of the care relationship between the nurse and the mentally ill patient lies a psychodynamic barrier, which operates to locate madness in the patient and sanity in the nurse. This is reflected at the organisational level such as in task construction and allocation. So, for example, contact between nurse and patient is organised by task (such as dispensing medication on a ward) rather than being organised around individual service users and being led by them. From a psychodynamic point of view, this is part of a culture of distance and control in which nurses are protected from emotional involvement with the mentally ill patient, and society is protected from being overwhelmed by, or infected with, madness (Hyde and Davies, 2004). At its worst, such a culture disenfranchises the patient, effectively prevents the patient from getting well and inducts new nurses into recursive practices of care which resist change. Hyde and Davies (2004) conclude their discussion by arguing that changes in performance and service-user involvement in the care of the mentally ill service-user will come about only when the psychodynamic subtext of anxiety and control is acknowledged. This would appear to require concurrent changes in societal attitudes towards mental illness and in the unacknowledged fantasies we have of our National Health Service's capacity to heal all illness or prolong life indefinitely.

Reflective point

Think about whether this argument can be applied in part or in whole to social services organisations. Is there a social services culture that regulates the emotional contact between social worker and service user?

These questions are discussed further in **Chapter Five** on teams in social work, where the conclusion is that the care relationship is indeed controlled to a degree in this way, with the unofficial discourse, official discourse and administrative practices tending to locate dependency, vulnerability or moral failure in the service user, and to locate moral right in the social worker. It is therefore possible to find a culture of care at work in the recursive practices of social services organisations, but it is one that can have both positive and negative consequences for the service user.

Gender and organisational culture

This chapter began with the assertion that organisations with a culture of care could buttress discriminatory practices. Gender is a key dimension of such practices. Wilson (2001) argues that all organisational cultures are gendered, insofar as they have rituals for identifying and subordinating workers – both women and men – in jobs perceived to be female, they have gendered enclaves and rituals for regulating power relations between men and women. Even in organisations where front-line service staff are female, such as social care organisations, there will be points of interface with men, and it is therefore useful to examine these power practices and other gendered aspects of the culture of social care organisations.

Maddock and Parkin (1993) identified six types of gendered culture in the public sector:

1. Gentleman's Club
2. Barrack Room
3. Locker Room
4. Gender Blind
5. Lip Service/Feminist Pretenders
6. Smart Macho.

The 'Gentleman's Club' culture was seen to be characterised by polite, civilised behaviour, patronising towards women, and by which women were kept in a subordinate place. Here, women survive if they conform. The 'Barrack Room' culture, by contrast, was seen to be characterised by an atmosphere of bullying, hostility towards identifiable difference and an authoritarian power culture within which women and other disadvantaged groups were rendered invisible.

The 'Locker Room' contained common assumptions and agreements between men; there was much talk about sex and sport, exaggerated body language, and women were excluded from the inner circle of men.

'Gender Blind' cultures assert that there is no difference between men and women. They thus ignore women's identity and reality, and do not see obstacles to women (which can in turn lead to the 'superwoman' syndrome). 'Lip Service/ Feminist Pretenders' cultures typically had good policies and equality experts, but oppressed groups vied for attention and resources, resulting in little change. Finally, 'Smart Macho' cultures, which according to Maddock and Parkin (1993), were commonly found in NHS management, are typically very competitive. Although overtly in favour of equal opportunities, the long hours culture and inflexible working patterns rendered equality impossible in practice.

Scourfield (2006) argues that social workers need to be aware of the gender narratives or assumptions enshrined in the organisational culture of child protection teams. If social workers can become aware of this, runs Scourfield's argument, then they have a chance of changing it. An example of this would be the assumption that poor women with few resources who are oppressed by violent male partners should be able to protect their children from a violent man when given an ultimatum to do so by child protection services. For Scourfield (2006) there is similarly a discourse about men in the child protection team, made up of pieces of feminist theory, government policy and popular imagery. It tends to see men either as incidental to the care of the child and therefore marginal to the social worker's engagement with the family, as victims of unemployment or, occasionally, as primary child-protecting parents taking responsibility where the mother has failed to put the child's needs before her own.

Scourfield's is an especially interesting approach to thinking about organisational culture, because it goes beyond the analysis of gendered organisational roles allotted to employees, and examines the roles the organisation gives to its customers, seeing these as embedded in the professional and organisational narratives of social services. Aside from the obvious criticism that Scourfield's own research can be seen as yet another such narrative, there is the misgiving that naming a narrative is by no means the same thing as changing it.

Identity and organisational culture

Moving on from discussion of the impact of gender on organisational culture, another aspect of organisational culture is the impact it has upon the identity of the individual.

Agatha Harrison, the first university welfare tutor in Britain, appointed to the social science department of the London School of Economics in 1917, famously loved nice clothes and took especial care of her appearance, sometimes appearing at public meetings in black velvet and with her red hair elaborately coiffured (Harrison, 1956). She deplored any tendency to look 'social workerly', as she termed it, although she was widely known as a social worker. What is interesting here is that as far back as 1917 social workers could apparently be recognised by their mode of dress, because this suggests that even amongst her first classes of welfare work students there was some sort of occupational culture of social work. While the link between the identity of the individual worker and her organisational setting is a complex one (Hatch and Schultz, 2004), the view of Hyde and Davies (2004) is that culture refers to any behaviour or belief held in common with others. Harvey (1980) noted that welfare workers in the 1890s were commonly recognisable by their dress, not least for fundraising purposes. Harvey has also pointed out that some welfare organisations such as The Salvation Army and the Women's Royal Voluntary Service still wear uniforms today. Pratt and Rafaeli (1997) have also referred to the 'uniformed' side of care work, highlighting some interesting research with nursing auxiliaries in a stroke rehabilitation setting. A manager in a rehabilitation unit wanted to introduce a culture of smart casual dress for staff in order to help patients adjust more easily to moving back into the community after treatment. However, auxiliary nurses in the unit resisted giving up the wearing of 'scrubs', an ostensibly surgical uniform. The researchers found that while the auxiliaries were the lowest paid workers in the unit and did the dirtiest jobs, wearing scrubs gave them a visual identity with theatre nurses who were a relatively high-status, high-pay group. Pratt and Rafaeli (1997) concluded that the relationship between individual identity and the culture of an organisational unit can be remarkably resistant to change.

Clothing can also provide significant clues to the deeply held beliefs about success and culture referred to earlier. Entire offices of similarly dressed women may reveal their commitment to a particular group conception of what they consider to be their organisational goals. Men do not find entry into these female cultures easy, often experiencing role strain (Simpson, 2005), and they will find ways of preserving masculinity within such occupations (Hall et al, 2007); Lupton (2006) reported that men in predominantly female occupations like social work sometimes use dress codes to emphasise their masculinity, with a preference for suits in some settings, suggesting an association with management and its more competitive, masculine culture. Male care workers commonly wear sports clothing or uniforms, choosing functional, military or sub-cultural haircuts, again perhaps seeking masculine associations within a female organisational culture; the beards with which male junior school teachers, playworkers, social workers and nurses equipped themselves in the 1970s became proverbial. Finally, some social workers still go on their rounds presenting their religious identity with symbols over their desks, in their cars, and even on their lapels. The broader issue is, as Alvesson and Willmott (2004) have pointed out, how the individual identity the worker receives from her organisational setting affects her professional practice. Does it, for example, restrict the range of her decision making? Clearly, though, social workers do not uncritically read off their identities from some monolithic organisational culture. Yet, as we have seen, 'watch your back' and 'blaming' cultures, 'safety procedure-ignoring' cultures and 'workaholic' cultures are readily recognised. Other cultures, such as those conducive to risk decision-making (possibly that of the learning organisation), or antithetical to it (the 'silo' culture, for example), may be less obvious (Westrum, 2004).

The culture of social work training

Buchanan and Huczynski (2004) used a training exercise in which readers of a narrative about becoming a bond trader on Wall Street were invited to identify the way in which the traders' training culture prepared them for life on the trading floor. Key phrases such as 'it's a jungle out there' were identified, along with a culture of bullying, machismo and anti-intellectualism.

Arguably, social work training also has a training culture of its own, which aims to prepare the worker for life in the social work organisational setting (an exercise at the end of this chapter invites the reader to consider what this might be). Research in this area is relatively thin and tends to focus upon the social organisation of training, such as communities of practice (Rogoff, 1990; Lave and Wenger, 1991; Wenger, 1998; Moore, 2008; and see **Chapter Seven** in this book). Nonetheless, it seems possible to identify such general features as self-criticism, criticism of other students' practice and values, commitment, and self-denial, in the training culture of this and other female professions (Jewkes, 1998). On practice placements, women can be treated in line with the culture or subculture of their placement organisation, and therefore variously as valuable additions to the team, as guests, as 'passing through', as excluded, as intruders, as marginal, or as a threat.

Conclusion

An organisational culture can be more obvious to a new employee, sensitised as she necessarily is to those around her, than the culture of the host society in which the organisation is embedded, even though there is an interchange between the two. The organisational culture can be experienced as supportive, as oppressive, or as conflicted. Culture can facilitate or undermine good social work practice. Organisational cultures and subcultures can display an amazing propensity to survive over time; despite change, underlying dynamics can constantly reassert themselves. It is possible to shift the centre of gravity of an organisation's culture by judicious hiring, firing, induction and supervision, perhaps in the process creating new oppositional subcultures or scepticism within the new culture. Change in culture can lead to more satisfied customers or clients, cementing it firmly to the organisation.

At worst 'organisational culture' is just too difficult to define (Kakabadse et al, 2004, p 188) and therefore too vague to discuss meaningfully. At best, the term 'organisational culture' conveniently summarises the employee's or service user's experience of their encounter with the organisation, much as a holiday or a show might be summarised in a conversation. Most of us will have experienced the warm glow that a sense that an organisation shares our own values can give, whether that organisation is just a wholefood store, a charity we support, or maybe a religious organisation. We have all probably also felt uncomfortable in organisations where the values were palpably not our own, in the employer we have left, or in the shops, businesses and restaurants we avoid. In that sense we have all been in the service user's shoes, if only to a limited extent.

> ▶**KEY LEARNING POINTS**
>
> - The formal structure and the history of the individual welfare organisation are the two main determinants of its culture.
> - The culture of a welfare organisation can either enshrine oppressive attitudes and buttress discriminatory, counter-productive and even dangerous practices, or it can facilitate openness, mutual care and service-user focus.
> - Individual workers can have a surprising influence upon the subculture of an office or service delivery unit.
> - Organisational culture is difficult to change, but developments such as service-user involvement can shift the organisational culture
> - The culture of the individual welfare organisation can influence social work relations with service users

▶SEMINAR ORIENTATION: CULTURES OF SOCIAL WORK TRAINING

Is there a culture specific to social work training settings within organisations, or is the concept of organisational culture too vague to be applied in this way? Consider if each of the following expectations can be detected in social work training:

*   going the extra mile, working out of hours, such as over holidays, at weekends and especially at lunchtime
*   demonstrating a concern for the client's needs before your own
*   willingness to explorie feelings, for example in supervision
*   displaying a readiness to reflect critically upon your own learning needs
*   showing a disregard for your own hardships in travelling to and from the placement
*   a 'can do' attitude to managing your own care responsibilities at home
*   an intuitive understanding of the appropriate dress code for the placement.

▶EXERCISE: THE CORNER

Read pages 68–85 of *The Corner* (1997) by David Simon and Ed Burns before discussing the following questions.

*   What is the dress code of the drug distribution organisation described in the extract?
*   What gender roles are offered to employees?
*   What was the 'Dealer's Code', and what imperatives overcame it?
*   What values did children subscribe to when they joined the organisation of the Corner?
*   What are the several classes of worker employed by the organisation?
*   What are the criteria for a successful career in the organisation?
*   What is likely to render an applicant ineligible for employment in the organisation?

CHAPTER SEVEN

Organisational learning: is a learning organisation a good place to work?

What you will learn in this chapter
- Origins of the concept of the learning organisation
- Criticisms of the learning organisation model
- How the learning organisation model is applicable to social work
- How to identify a learning organisation
- Communities of practice and their applicability to social work organisations

Introduction

What is a learning organisation? This may be a useful figure of speech, but is an organisation an entity which can learn?

Morgan (2006) has described learning organisation theory using a metaphor in which the organisation is conceptualised as a brain. Substantively, it is a particular type of organisational structure which enables and facilitates individual and team learning in order to increase organisational responsiveness and efficiency.

The concept of 'the learning organisation' is a relatively recent idea, however, drawing on the recognition in the 1970s of 'knowledge' as a key resource of the organisation (Drucker, 1974). In today's ever-changing world, it may appear obvious that organisations must understand customer need in order to have competitive advantage and must know about new technologies to be more efficient, but this was not the case in an earlier industrial era.

Towards the end of the long post-war economic boom, Schön (1973) and Argyris (Argyris and Schön, 1974, 1978) saw the rapid technological advances (in particular the commercial use of the microprocessor from 1974 onwards) as an important driver towards organisational change, but also observed that it led to a redundancy of existing knowledge. The renewal of knowledge is therefore necessary for 're-tooling' or to make use of these new technologies:

> We must [...] become adept at learning. We must become able not only to transform our institutions, in response to changing situations and requirements; we must invent and develop institutions which are 'learning systems', that is to say, systems capable of bringing about their own continuing transformation. (Schön, 1973, p 28)

An industry must develop the theoretical knowledge underpinning technological advances or the transformation of processes not only in response to change but *before* making the advances, or staff will lack the ability to operate new processes efficiently. Given the end goal of efficiency, organisational learning (and the learning organisation) can be seen as simply the more recent phases of scientific management (see **Chapter One**), although they are considered by many to be more than this. The learning organisation model (TLO) was developed from these organisational learning theories by Senge (1990) but can be distinguished from them (Hodgkinson and Sparrow, 2002) and will be explored at the beginning of this chapter.

In Britain, TLO also coincided nicely with the Investors in People standard (a framework for skills development in business), which launched in 1991. Following a government report which had identified the poor skills profile of British workers compared to continental firms, the then Secretary of State for Employment, Michael Howard, sold the idea of a 'standard' to the Confederation of British Industry. Many big firms qualified immediately and Investors in People still sets the standards for good practice in the UK.

The TLO model also continues to be popular (see for example, Rylatt, 2003). You will probably be familiar with ideas developed from TLO such as 'smart' working and learning, passing information back from the point of service delivery, building organisations that empower employees to learn and to share their learning, and using intrinsic motivation to achieve efficacy rather than extrinsic rewards (see **Chapter Two**).

It is not difficult to see the implications of a learning organisation argument for social work: changes in service user need arising from demographic changes, immigration, social issues such as unemployment, new forms of substance abuse, obesity, and so on, all change the context for welfare organisations. Knowledge and learning to inform practice are also key elements of strategic management.

Senge: the learning organisation

Johnson (2010) asserts that, although the components of the learning organisation can be traced back to the 1970s and earlier, nonetheless Senge (1990) remains the 'guru' most readily associated with the idea. However, he rejects the notion that it is a management fad, and prefers to think of it as a social movement. The TLO model was outlined in Peter Senge's *The fifth discipline* (1990). TLO is made up of five disciplines:

1. Personal mastery: personal goals.
2. Mental models: reflection and inquiry.
3. Shared vision: group commitment.
4. Team learning: collective thinking.
5. Systems thinking: understanding interdependency and feedback.

Figure 7.1: The learning organisation model

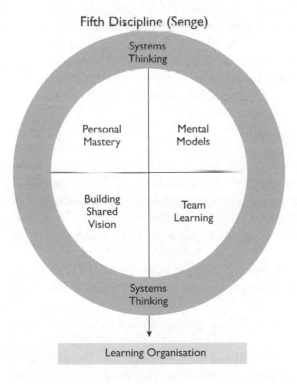

Source: Adapted from Senge, 1990.

Senge (1990) believed TLO to be a theory of human potential and as such it is also a theory of motivation (see **Chapter Two**). TLO is experiential in focus and takes a social constructivist view of organisational life (Berger and Luckmann, 1967), rather than the objectifying, rational–scientific and managerialist focus of preceding scientific management theories. Overall, it is possible to see the shift from the essentially mechanistic metaphor applied to organisations by Taylor (see **Chapter One**) to the organismic metaphors applied by Senge (1990) and others as a 'paradigm change' (Kuhn, 1970; Morgan, 2006). The later paradigm acknowledges some features of organisations which are continuous with the earlier paradigm, but approaches them in a different way. This is perhaps why the features of TLO seem so familiar and yet are somehow features of a new organisational world that is not understood within the otherwise excellent analyses of organisational behaviour in the pre-war period (eg Gilbreth, 1911; Taylor, 1911; Ford, 1922).

There is also a sense in which TLO unites layers of previous organisational theories. For example, it incorporates the ideas of Drucker (1955) and of Peters and Waterman (1982), linking the 'vision' of the organisation with a process of continuous change in the organisation's understanding of itself and individuals' and teams' understanding of their business environment. Senge's (1990) ideal seems to be of a direct relationship between customer need and employee action: the need is anticipated or discovered, this produces learning, which results in production and delivery of the most appropriate product (or service) in the shortest possible time.

This may seem to be a very capitalist approach not suited to welfare organisations. There is a useful caution in the work of Peters (1987), however, that applies well to this model: it may be a bad idea to impose a model that has worked in another organisation on your own organisation and expect it to produce similar results. Each organisation must grow its own learning organisation.

Criticisms of the learning organisation

Although employees like the sense of self-development that TLO brings, there is little empirical research on the success of this model. It can also be difficult to implement fully. The organisational change required can be expensive and, 'systems thinking', in particular, can require a lot of time spent on feedback and measurement, which employees may not consider a priority, or in social work as the real welfare task.

In practice therefore this model often boils down to the provision of learning opportunities for staff, personal development plans and training and socialisation into shared values.

Reflective point

In a period of financial crisis, how realistic or achievable are even these basic aspects of TLO, such as training opportunities and effective use of personal development plans?

Systems thinking is also problematic because, although it is an holistic approach which looks at how all aspects of the organisation influence one another, systems theories (such as Parsons, 1951) are also functionalist. Functionalism provides a good basis for understanding the complexity of organisations, but it presupposes an overall aim of stability. Systems theories will therefore view conflict as a transition to a state of equilibrium. They will look at how equilibrium can be modelled, rather than analysing the conflict itself. Systems thinking is therefore of limited value where conflict is more or less permanent in an organisation. So, for example, the rift running through a service unit between the deputy and staff on one hand, and the unit manager on the other, may be seen as a temporary problem of fragmented values in the organisation rather than as a structural feature of such service units.

It is also possible that individuals in an organisation do not learn best through the use of personal goals, experiments, feedback loops or double learning loops (that is, learning about the learning process itself). The TLO model does not integrate other methods of learning, for example emulating colleagues or the slow accretion of experience.

A final criticism, made by Hodgkinson and Sparrow (2002), is that tacit individual and group knowledges and learning approaches, such as those that are found in communities of practice (which are discussed below), are not really comprised within the TLO model, yet these unreflected knowledges continue to exist within learning organisations.

Learning in social work organisations

When thinking about the impact of TLO on social work organisations we must consider that (to paraphrase Drucker, 1955) the biggest problem of organisations today is that of how to turn information into knowledge. Feedback loops and evidence-based practice do not in themselves constitute knowledge; what is more important is how the mass of information impinging on the social worker can be turned into *usable* knowledge, that is, intelligent practice. As Gould and Baldwin (2004) have observed, this is the root of the focus on reflective practice in social work in recent years, and the drive to incorporate this into sound supervision and teamwork.

Gould and Baldwin (2004) argued that a number of separate influences have led to the adoption of TLO models in social services settings. First, a fast-moving and globalising business environment has required all organisations to confront the prospect of continuous change and adaptation, rather than the periodic strategic change or goal-setting identified by earlier analysts. To this can be added the various policy initiatives designed to make the personal social services more responsive and sensitive to service user need and to encourage collaborative working. In social work there have been moves towards a TLO model as a result of child protection inquiries, for example, and their recommendations for improving practice. In particular, the Laming Inquiry highlighted the organisational context of individual social work accountability, forcing organisational structure, communication and, most importantly, organisational learning, onto the agenda. These specific social work drivers have combined with the development of organisations more broadly to push social work organisations towards TLO. Gray et al (2010) argue that there may be one or more different TLO cultures present in a social services department at any one time, and identify three distinct models of TLO:

1. Profession-led TLO developed as part of a professional learning culture, in which learning and development are seen as a professional responsibility. A key feature is that it is led by some requirement for or expectation of continuing professional registration, linked to skill updates, such as is the case in nursing, occupational therapy and social work.
2. A management-led learning culture, in which learning and development are directed towards organisational goals and are driven by managers. In these situations strategic organisational change may involve restructuring the entire organisation along TLO lines.
3. A humanistic learning culture, which is focused upon personal growth and development.

Clearly, the distinction between profession-led and management-led TLO has consequences for the social worker. If TLO culture is profession-led within an organisation which has strategic objectives that are not entirely congruent with TLO models, social work might feel like an enclave within the wider organisation. Gray et al's (2010) humanistic learning culture is reminiscent of managerial culture in social work half a century ago.

Lambley (2009) and others have argued that a culture of organisational learning is not only desirable but also essential for the development of social work staff and therefore for optimum supervision. Yet the extent to which a team learning culture can be fostered by the social worker, senior practitioner or manager, will depend partly upon its compatibility with the wider organisational culture. This is what we mean when we talk about cultural 'obstacles' to supervision (**Chapter Six**): the personal and professional development of the supervisee depends on an organisational culture that enables this.

Another aspect of social work practice impacted by organisational learning is that of evaluation (Shaw, 2004). In social work, evaluation has tended to be something undertaken by organisations periodically to assess the efficacy of particular social welfare programmes. In this guise, it not infrequently precedes structural change imposed externally. A TLO approach to evaluation, however, places the emphasis upon continuous evaluation and modification. This would appear to be a positive route to continuous improvements, but in practice, as Shaw (2004) notes, this can lead to small, incremental changes which may fall short of external bodies' expectations of organisational change, and indeed of service users' and social workers' desire for greater transformation of services. Perhaps what distorts the system most of all in relation to social work is time: delays inherent within the feedback loops and double-learning loops create a disjunction between the feedback from the service user, through learning, to changes in the planning and delivery of services, and it is this that in the long run may be the most difficult thing to change.

How do you know if you work in a learning organisation?

Referring back to the diagram of the learning organisation in Figure 7.1, it should be possible to see a continuous loop between the mission of the organisation and the learning of the individual employee. The social worker's perception of the organisation and its purpose is in line with the mission; the social worker's experiential learning from the service user and intervention is shared with the team, and the team's changed understanding loops with organisational change via the evolving mission. In practice, the social worker in an incipient learning organisation might encounter any, all or none of the following:

- Trials and experimental improvements: the block contracting of nursing home or residential home beds by NHS–local authority social services consortia could be considered an example of trialling improvements.
- Participative policy making: 'roadshows' and other types of staff forum may not be participative in any meaningful sense, but e-voting on organisational issues such as mission statements and core business descriptions could be considered a step in the right direction.
- Information sharing: IT has been used to provide information to front-line staff for many years now; evidence-based practice is also based on information sharing.
- Informative accounting: for example giving front-line staff information about the budget, what it is, how much is being spent and by whom.
- Internal exchange: effective sharing of information in inter-agency settings such as in hospital social work teams, or NHS deaths circulars being shared with social services offices so that cases can be definitively closed.
- Reward flexibility: perhaps linking excellence ratings in social services departments to bonus payments; some agencies supplying social workers already operate bonus systems.
- Enabling structures: for example reconstituting teams to meet task requirements, with people being moved around based on skills.
- Boundary workers becoming an information source: the regular completion of statistical returns by front-line workers is now well established in many teams and service units.
- Inter-organisational learning: for example, joint NHS and social work training.
- A learning climate: lots of manager feedback to staff and regular team meetings, supervision, reflective practice, team sharing of practice and reflection within interdisciplinary teams, learning from and with service user groups, shared team interpretation of and feedback on policy.
- Self-development opportunities: High visibility training opportunities available to all, with linked progression and regular learning and career reviews, as well as staff taking responsibility for their own learning (Pedler et al, 1997).

Communities of practice

While TLO became noticeable in British welfare organisations from the mid-1990s, by this time American corporations had moved on to experiment with Communities of Practice (Brown and Duguid, 1991) and other models of organisation. Lave and Wenger (1991) draw on the writings of Bourdieu to argue that learning is a process of participation in a community of practice (CoP).

The more mastery the apprentice learner gains over the language and technologies of the community, the closer they move to the centre of that community. Learning, in this sense, refers to a practice of increasing participation and mastery over the resources of the community.

Moore (2008) refers to the potential of CoP to move away from 'linear' models of expert–student learning to 'bi-directional' teaching and learning, with both groups contributing to the community's knowledge base.

Also, Moore notes the 'dialogic' exploration of alternative ways to solve problems in a CoP and, perhaps most important for our argument here, to the ability of a CoP to bestow 'legitimacy' upon newcomers, enabling them 'to make mistakes, stumble, and commit violations as a part of the learning process' (Moore, 2008, p 596). This is not to say that students do not fail, but rather that within the CoP model it is possible to acknowledge that others within the CoP acknowledge and learn from failure themselves; to reframe mistakes as learning opportunities.

Figure 7.2: Communities of practice

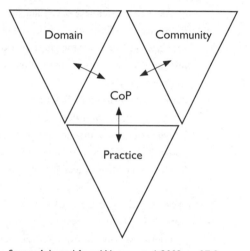

Source: Adapted from Wenger et al, 2002, pp 27-9.

Lesser and Storck (2001) argue that CoPs are a form of organisational social capital: they are part of the value of the organisation and enhance its performance.

However, on the one hand, participation in a 'success' culture leaves the real possibility of participants learning the language as a technological resource without any corresponding engagement. On the other hand, the experience of failure may lead to a fall from a cultural community and is potentially a strong motivator for reflective engagement with the meaning – existential and personal – of the language games in which the students are engaged (Wittgenstein, 1968).

From this, the contention is two-fold. First, that there is a need to foster such an alternative culture of success if we are to take the idea of failure seriously, that is to reconceptualise social work training as a CoP process, within which failure is acknowledged as an active part of everyone's learning in the CoP. Second, there is a need to examine the very personal and existential dimensions of failing (Heidegger, 1927; Jaspers, 1931, 1932; Cocteau, 1937) to consider what such an alternative culture might look like. (There are motivational consequences of such a culture and these can usefully be linked to the discussion of motivation in social services organisations in **Chapter Two**.)

As Stamps (1997) has noted, CoP looks at first sight like a plea for more on-the-job training and less classroom learning; it is not. If this were a cost-cutting initiative it would fail, because on-the-job training has been shown to be a more expensive option than formal training courses (Stamps, 1997). This is partly because CoPs cannot be created (Wenger, 1998): you can acknowledge their existence; you can bring other groups of employees into contact with them and hope for the best. Some organisational settings will not possess strong CoPs, which means that if they are being relied upon for training employees on the job, the backup of classroom-based learning may be even more important. This is especially important in social work and also goes some way to explaining why one social work department can turn student after student into successful social workers, whereas others withdraw from training altogether following a couple of poor student experiences. Factors such as workloads and staffing levels must also be considered in making such a statement, but we can acknowledge that some offices are just better places for student learning than others.

Communities of practice in social work

This model of learning has gained increasing recognition in pedagogical circles (for example, Rogoff, 1990; Matusov et al, 2005) and for its applicability to social work education (for example Moore, 2008) Its potential application in social work is particularly interesting considering the current regulation of practice learning by the professional bodies of British social work, and the models of learning within social work regulation. By repositioning social work education away from a monological, hierarchical model of teaching and learning, the CoP approach lends itself to a dialogical, open-ended and flat, 'I–thou' model, of the kind advocated by, for example, Irving and Young (2006) as a model for social work practice itself. This might bring social work education more in line with the empowerment perspectives to which the profession currently aspires in practice.

While professional regulatory bodies of social work have been concerned to ensure that procedures for failing students are operated in a fair and anti-discriminatory fashion, it seems reasonable to raise the wider question of the status and significance of failure, both in the lives of social workers and social work students and in social work itself, and the social policies which underpin it. Arguably, longstanding social work aims are ill-served by the existence of a 'success' culture, since it places the social worker and the recipient at opposite poles of a construct which is detrimental to the recipient and self-defeating to the social worker. One way forward may be to acknowledge and accept failure rather than disowning it (Jaspers, 1931; Schlipp, 1957; Thyssen, 1957), so as not only to recognise it but also to understand its role in the lives of service recipients (Cocteau, 1937). This could reinforce the sense of shared humanity to which social work has allied itself historically, rather than simply reinforcing the 'in group–out group' dynamics of a success culture (Stretch, 1967; Sinsheimer, 1969; Thompson, 1992). By conceptualising the training process as a CoP, failure can be seen as part of a dialogical process in which everyone learns. In this way it may be possible to move towards an organisational and training culture within which mistakes are more likely to be owned and used as learning opportunities, by tutors as well as by students (Milner and O'Byrne, 1986).

Conclusion

It appears that TLO is a good place for a social worker to work, and the appeal of TLO approaches in social work are not difficult to understand: it is participative, democratic, anti-authoritarian and, in principle, it is empowering to service users and front-line staff. Indeed Higham (2009) has argued that, together with post-qualifying training, moving to a TLO format is a major way in which social services organisations can improve the recruitment and retention of social workers. Furthermore, as TLO is experiential and takes a social constructivist view of organisational life (Berger and Luckmann, 1967), viewing the organisation as a shared reality that is made and remade continuously by its participating actors, TLO accords the actions and meaning-construction of front-line staff and service users greater importance within the social work organisation. This resonates not only with the Code of Practice and legal requirements, but also with studies such as those of Lipsky (1980) which have found that front-line public service workers interpret central policy for themselves anyway. Finally, there is a pleasing synergy between TLO's double-loop learning and the importance of reflective practice enshrined in current models of good social work.

Yet, as Gould and Baldwin (2004) have argued, TLO language has increasingly been co-opted into organisational policy statements, without a corresponding shift away from a top-down, managerialist form of social services delivery. Baldwin therefore sees the shift to bottom-up-transformed, co-operative, flexible, learning and service-user-responsive forms of social services delivery as more apparent than real. The resilience of bureaucratic forms in the organisational structure of local government should also not be under-estimated, whether they are viewed as a hindrance to the development of TLO or whether they are viewed as a buffer against managerialism and marketisation (Schofield, 2001). Gould and Baldwin (2004) nonetheless remain optimistic about the appeal and possibilities of TLO in social work organisations, despite cutbacks arising from the current financial crisis affecting many local authority social services departments.

Finally, Bissell and Sullivan (2012) argue that the organisational learning models need to be balanced by a positive conception of failure if the potential gains from failure audits are not to be lost (Carson and Bain, 2008).

▶KEY LEARNING POINTS

- Organisational learning and TLO models offer ways of explaining the role of the organisation in knowledge creation and the facilitation of learning
- The TLO model is a popular management strategy that is also widely implemented in social services organisations
- Research points to the popularity of a learning organisation approach with social work staff, although there are criticisms of the approach, especially its use in social work organisations
- The wider engagement aspects of TLO models are in line with the philosophy of user-led services, but research suggests that service change may be disappointing
- Community of practice models offer a helpful alternative for learning in social work organisations, but an acceptance of failure as part of a learning process is necessary

▶EXERCISE: THE MAZE

In teams of three (or more), attempt the following maze exercise. First draw a maze and make ten copies (for each person who will be attempting the maze); you will also need a stop-watch and graph paper. The first person attempts to draw a route through the maze, the second person times how long it takes to plot a route through the maze, while the third records the time on a graph. This is repeated ten times, each time on a fresh copy of the maze.

The third person then constructs a learning curve from the times plotted on the graph.

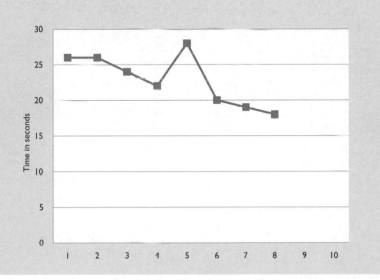

Additional team members can also attempt the maze to create different learning curves. Any exercise based upon task repetition to illustrate the learning curve concept is useful here.

How far do the learning 'curves' produced by different individuals resemble one another? Is there a typical learning line for this task? Can you observe any affects on the learning curve, such as expectation or interruption? To what extent can the model of learning in this exercise be considered applicable to some social work skills?

CHAPTER EIGHT

Leadership and management: is a social work style of management possible?

What you will learn in this chapter

- What management is and what managers do
- Different forms of management including devolved and self-management
- Attributes of managers
- Management styles including gender issues
- The complexity of management in social services settings
- Importance of empowerment

Introduction

To say that organisational structure in social services is policy driven on a fairly short cycle would not be over-stretching the point. As recently as a decade ago, Harlow (2000) was asking if the then diminishing numbers of recruits to social work courses signalled a decline of social work as a career for women. Its status as a profession subjected to occasional ridicule and its public image damaged, social work was viewed by Harlow (2000) as being 'taken over by male managers'. Moreover, these 'male managers' were sometimes without formal social work qualifications and were unwittingly closing off career opportunities for women, while at the same time were accused of subjecting the social work role to an emptying of caring content. Although the public image of social work continues to face challenges, only two decades on, recruitment is not, for the moment, a problem. The reasons for this are complex and the situation at the mercy of policy changes, but the debate about professionalisation no longer strikes at the core of social work's organisational problems. Aspects of management have progressively devolved downwards in the flatter welfare organisations of the twenty-first century, bringing with them not only, as Harlow (2000) noted, the awareness of budgetary constraints, but also the idea of the implementation of policy and of organisational change as responsibilities of social workers themselves.

Commenting on recent trends in the management of social care organisations, Hafford-Letchfield et al (2008) observed an increase in the tensions between social work values and a rather narrow managerialism with a focus on planning, targets and goal setting, and distributed management. Given the vulnerability of social services to cycles of short-term changes in social policy (Williams, 2001), it will be more useful in this chapter to examine current trends in social work management, as Hafford-Letchfield has done for the social care sector (Hafford-Letchfield et al, 2008), rather than to seek distinctive attributes of the management role *per se*.

This chapter will therefore critically examine various theories of management and concepts about who managers are and what they do, and consider recent trends in social services management and the social work role.

What is management?

In analysing the role and responsibilities of the manager at the end of the 1960s, Mintzberg (1973) produced a now well-known compromise between two approaches to analysing management. These were, on the one hand, that of identifying distinctive management attributes, and, on the other, that of describing existing management practices. Before Mintzberg's 'action research' approach to what managers actually did with their time, the seven core activities of managerial jobs (something like the Key Roles currently used in social work training) (according to Smith and Davidson, 1991) were:

1. Planning
2. Organising
3. Staffing
4. Deciding
5. Controlling
6. Reporting
7. Budgeting.

With his research into the activities of executives in *The nature of managerial work* (1973), Mintzberg produced findings that remain relevant to understanding management today. He described the core management task as fragmented, superficial and caught in a loop of fragmentation and superficiality. A 'loop' is created in which the fast, superficial, damage-limiting responses needed to react to immediate crises leave the manager unable to tackle the underlying problems, which can go on to generate ever more problems for the manager to handle. Mintzberg's (1973) observations of managers' time budgets (that is, of the amount of time spent upon particular types of task) bear comparison with the time budgets of social workers. For example, the reactive nature of much management work, the emphasis upon networking behaviour, interruptions and the consequent fragmentation in dealing with any particular problem, are all familiar elements of the social worker's role, and will be returned to later in this chapter.

Some of Mintzberg's (1973) findings are no longer relevant though; for example the significance of mail and written communication in the manager's working day has clearly been overtaken by almost universal use of email in business.

Mant (1979) questioned whether some management attributes had not become unreasonably and unrealistically fetishised in Britain, partly as a result of American managerial language being misunderstood. Mant disagreed that managerial work was more important than the work of others in the organisation, and disputed the view that economic and social progress depended upon managers.

These unrealistic expectations of managers, which, as Mant asserted, began with Burnham's *Managerial revolution* (1942), were not dispelled until Senge (1990) and others partially decentred the manager in what was in effect a more distributed view of organisational responsibility (see **Chapter Seven**).

Distribution of power and responsibility

There seems little doubt that there has been a downward distribution of some management functions in recent years. Indeed, the move towards the hollowing out of public sector organisations, and the consequent disappearance of some layers of managers, has led to 'distributed management' and the increasing devolution of many of the tasks of the manager onto employees, including social workers.

> **Reflective point**
> Look back at the list of the seven activities of management and think about the roles of social workers in relation to those activities.

Front-line social workers may now have responsibility for:

* significant amounts of care planning and even service planning;
* organising their own workload;
* inductions for new staff and mentoring;
* decision making of a varied and non-routine kind;
* controlling access to services;
* reporting of information and feedback to other departments; and
* working within detailed budgets.

The devolved, distributed management of today's social service unit (Watson, 2002) attaches very little real power to many management functions although, as Mintzberg (1973) noted, power is far from everything in management. Actual decision making, while an important management activity (Simon, 1945), does not engross the lion's share of managers' time. Leadership is also an aspect of management that is relatively rarely called upon (Mintzberg, 1973); also, leadership can be exercised by employees at all levels, depending upon the situation (Hughes and Waring, 2007).

In the flatter, distributed management organisation of present-day social services, management functions such as information gathering for senior management, implementation of policy, liaison with other agencies, 'figureheading', and adapting to service user need, are all now part of the routine or occasional functions of front-line social workers. Nor are these the only changes in managerial work since Mintzberg's 1973 study. The function of disseminating information among team members and colleagues is now understood to be something that not only occurs informally but is perhaps more effective when done in this way (Lave and

Wenger, 1991). Dealing with staff conflict, harassment and behaviour has now become the devolved responsibility of everyone, thanks to policies to manage harassment, smoking and alcohol in the workplace, and the self-reporting of accidents and absences.

Self-management

As Grey (2007) has pointed out, this has also led to self-management, which has been enshrined within the Key Roles and the Capabilities Framework for social work practice. Public service organisations, increasingly like business organisations, are ever-changing machines, in which a growing penumbra of temporary agency staff are pressed to greater efficiency, self-managing and even leading change (Buchanan, 2003), in shifting, networking teams (Grey, 2007). Managers, where they operate, tend not to see themselves as managers anyway, but as change leaders: what Grey calls 'hypermanagers', or managers in the new, fast style who operate in organisations in which continuous restructuring is the *modus operandi*. It is perhaps also true that the term 'manager' has now come to be used for a much wider variety of administrative functions (such as that of care manager), attaching to it implications of bureaucracy that are inconsistent with the image of the flatter, faster, flexible organisation. This is not to say that the control function of public sector organisations has been sacrificed along with middle managers; quite the opposite. Continuous change requires ever more responsive control.

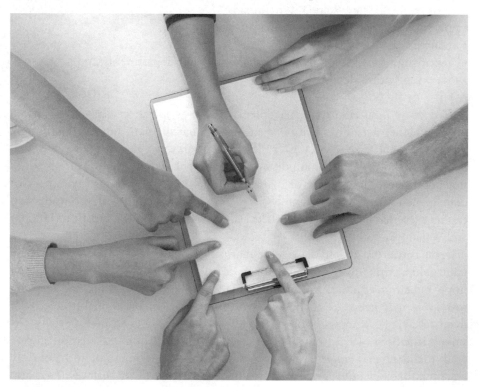

Peters (1987) advocated the self-managing team, and the retraining of the first-line manager as a supervisor or mentor, effectively increasing the span of control of the next tier of management but supporting a more empowered front-line worker. Given recent recommendations for the reform of social work which advocate intensive supervision and mentoring for newly qualified social workers, Peters' model may yet find a new lease of life.

Attributes of managers

Blake and Mouton (1964) developed a three-variable model, which distinguished managers according to their relationship skills, task skills and effectiveness. The value of this was that it underlined the fact that no one of these dimensions necessarily implied any of the others: just because a manager has good people skills we cannot assume that she has task skills or is an effective manager. Being an effective manager is not necessarily incompatible with relationship skills, but it is possible to be a resoundingly bad manager in several ways all at the same time!

Psychological approaches to management

At a time when the public were just beginning to suspect that senior public sector managers were neither universally principled nor unimpeachably competent (Booker, 1970), Drucker (1959) challenged what he perceived to be rule-bound bureaucratic departmental isolationism and made a very timely call for improvement. This improvement was through the 'personal development' school of management training which, along with 'sensitisation', third-force psychology and other related developments in the late 1950s and 1960s (Fast, 1970), formed the basis of psychological approaches to management. The 'great man' approach to management skills, popularised in the sometimes anecdotal styles of Barnard (1948), Page (1972) and Peters and Waterman (1982), underpins the case study approach that remains a popular teaching method in social work training, underlining the perennial popularity of concrete examples of good (and bad) practice. Mintzberg (1973) criticised the anecdotal approach on the grounds that it can be difficult to extract general principles.

If we consider how significant transference can be in client–worker relationships, it becomes clear that the psychodynamics of management and supervision are well worth examining (Bower, 2005). In *The structures and dynamics of organizations and groups* (Berne, 1963), Berne applied psychodynamic theory to organisational analysis. In particular, he looked at the concepts of Id, Ego and Superego and how they appear as Child, Adult and Parent 'ego states' in transactions between individuals in management and leadership interactions. Berne looked for bipolar and triangular relationships in organisations, and found that poor communication in organisations was often characterised by these conflicting ego states. His finding that conflicting ego states were also repeated down the hierarchy of large organisations helps to explain the disarming sensation that, no matter what we do, we seem to end up repeating the same patterns of relationships over and over again at work.

More recently Goleman (1995) identified skills related to engaging with others' emotions, as well as expressing one's own, and later connected these with organisational behaviour (Goleman, 2002). It proved possible to map these skills of 'emotional intelligence' onto management competencies.

Figure 8.1: Emotional intelligence for management

Dimension	Is the dimension a personal competence or a social competence?	What competencies are associated with this dimension?
Self-awareness	Personal	Emotional awareness Accurate self-assessment Self-confidence
Self-management	Personal	Self-control Transparency (Trustworthiness) Adaptability Achievement Initiative Optimism
Social awareness	Social	Empathy Organisational awareness Service
Relationship management	Social	Inspirational leadership Influence Developing others Change catalyst Conflict management Building bonds Teamwork and collaboration

Source: Goleman, 1998, 2002.

Given Berne's (1963) findings it is not surprising to find emotional intelligence advocated as a skill for managers (Caruso and Salovey, 2004). It is also unsurprising to find it advocated as a core skill in social work (Howe, 2008). However, research conducted by Moss et al (2006) which looked at whether 'emotionally intelligent' managers were less critical and detached with their extroverted and ambitious employees found no evidence to support better management practice from emotionally intelligent managers.

Masculisation of management

Roper (1994) observed a 'masculinisation' of management (which led to a masculinisation of classical organisational behaviour theory more broadly), which he views as having two proximal causes. First, the early lionisation of physical labour in primary industries, adopted as a coping response to the brutalisation of work, led managers to adopt similar forms of exaggerated masculinity to reinforce their legitimacy, removing supposedly 'feminine' traits (which will be discussed in more detail below) from the management role. Second, the practice of recruiting managers from the officer and non-commissioned officers of demobilised armies after the Second World War led to an infusion of 'military' masculinity to the human relations movement (Odiorne, 1965). It is interesting to note that this 'military' aspect of management behaviour was considered to be so self-evident, that James in his book *Business wargames* (1985) wondered why no one had previously written a book about the parallels between war and business strategies.

Management styles

A good way of thinking about the impact of different leadership and management styles is to imagine and compare the leadership styles of, say, Bruce Willis's mining engineer in the movie *Armageddon* with that of Meryl Streep's fashion magazine editor in *The devil wears Prada*. In these films, there is a stark contrast between task-oriented leadership (*Armageddon*) and personality-focused leadership (*The devil wears Prada*). This (and examples from many other films) can offer a helpful illustration of social–psychological theories in this area of organisational behaviour to which we will return below.

Practice example: management styles

Abida Hussein, a newly qualified social worker, is sent by an agency to cover a maternity leave vacancy in Springfield Area Office. She gets on well in the intake team, and is particularly valued for her work with families for whom English is a second language. The team leader is sensitive to Abida's needs as a newly qualified worker, making sure she has an induction to the team and drawing attention to her status at team meetings. She sees Abida regularly for supervision, and a proportion of this is taken up with attention to Abida's childcare arrangements and her experience of social work.

After twelve weeks the social worker for whom Abida was covering returns to work part-time and Abida is moved to Shelbyville intake team within the same local authority. This team has two members off sick, one of whom has been on leave for some time; all the remaining team members work part-time. Although she is valued for her contribution to this team, it takes much longer to get to know the members of the team. Also, although the manager of the team schedules supervision meetings for every three weeks, the manager is clearly under pressure to fit in everyone's supervision and the supervision meetings are spent discussing the most risky cases. Team meetings are similarly taken up with announcements of policy changes and consequent changes to procedures.

Abida meets up with a member of the Springfield team, and when she does she contrasts the different approaches of the two team leaders.

Beyond their job roles, management style is the main way in which employees evaluate their managers. Style has replaced the notion of personality and personality clash as a way of talking about management–staff relations. Whereas within earlier thinking about managers, personality was something that the manager was stuck with, linked to the idea that managers are born and not made, management style and behaviours can be changed by training or by management counsellors.

In the post-war industrial era Fleishman and Harris (1962), among others, examined leadership behaviours that reduced employee grievances and turnover. They interviewed several hundred clerks and asked them to rate their supervisors and identified two key factors: consideration and the tendency to initiate structure. They found that employees were more likely to accept structure, and tightening of structure, from managers who were deemed to be considerate. Conversely, employees experienced the structuring behaviour of those perceived to be job-focused supervisors as threatening. Interestingly, however, they concluded that to be rated low on *both* styles rendered a manager more unpopular than if they were rated high on job-focus. This implies that if your supervisor is unable to use an empowering management style, the next best thing is to be rated highly on job focus.

Tannenbaum and Schmidt: democratic and autocratic styles

One criticism of Fleishman and Harris's (1962) research is that it perhaps underestimates the impact of some aspects of context. At around the same time Tannenbaum and Schmidt (1958) analysed what they called democratic (ie consultative) and autocratic (ie top-down) styles and argued that good team leaders can adapt their style to the situation, as long as *overall* they are perceived to be democratic and capable of engaging with feelings. Managers may choose to shift between a democratic or an autocratic style dependent partly upon the employee (Tannenbaum and Schmidt, 1958): some workers have a lower tolerance of ambiguity than others, for example, and benefit from clearer directions. If you want to be managed democratically, you must demonstrate your independence, expertise, and an expectation of making your own decisions within defined limits.

Later researchers in the mid-1960s broke Tannenbaum and Schmidt's two styles down further into four styles:

- Exploitative–autocratic (never delegates);
- Benevolent–authoritative (condescending);
- Participative (listens); and
- Democratic (trusts).

Perhaps needless to say, retention and productivity were found to be better with the participative and democratic styles.

Mintzberg (1973), however, argued that far too much time had been devoted by social psychologists and others to management style and to autocratic and empowering styles in particular. He was certainly right that this is a crude dichotomisation of a small part of complex manager behaviour, yet, as Hafford-Letchfield (2008) has noted, the social care code of values is potentially compromised by autocratic and similar styles of management. This being so, research devoted to autocratic and empowering management styles is of immediate relevance to social workers.

Personalised and socialised power

A different 'management style' construct is offered by McClelland and Burnham (1976). They distinguished managers who wanted personal loyalty from their staff from those who wanted loyalty to the organisation. This can be described as personalised power or socialised power. Managers who seek personal power sometimes want to dominate those around them, exercising power impulsively or may seek advancement at the expense of others. Managers with socialised power aim to help others to understand their jobs in the light of organisational goals.

Management styles and gender

Wilson (2003) has argued that the participative, democratic style of women managers has been positively exploited not only in largely female occupations like social work but also in the private sector. Buchanan and Huczynski (2004) also suggest that current trends in management are moving towards more and more informal, empowering management styles. These participative and empowering methods are core skills used in social work, to the extent that it can be argued that social work skills are moving into business (Caruso and Salovey, 2004). The 'women's language' research is also relevant here (Coates, 2009), and Williams (2000) asks if the supposedly female 'ethic of care' might be something about which women should change perceptions.

The idea of intrinsically gendered characteristics may be flawed, however, in line with Butler's (1990) argument that gender is a performance rather than an essence. Supposedly 'female' and 'male' management styles are therefore also a performance, and there is nothing intrinsically female or male about them. In her study of women managers in a north of England local government service Maddock (1999) found the women had a detailed managerial approach which fits with the stereotype of the micro-managing female manager. Maddock's (1999) assertion that male managers appear to turn away from some of the detail of the work rings true and is in accordance with Mintzberg's (1973) findings about the superficiality of much of the work performed by the (male) managers he studied. However, it is debatable whether this putatively female detailed management approach is actually an essential gender characteristic; rather, it is a 'performance' in response to a perceived lack of power (Kanter, 1977).

Despite this view, research continues to focus upon gender-distinctive features of leadership. For example, Bartunek et al (2000) argued that woman-led teams of women display characteristic patterns of authority relations. In particular, internal leadership opportunities tended to be rotated and the group coordinator's focus tended to be shifted to external relations. Perhaps in part because of the gendered nature of communication (see **Chapter Three**), women tend to fare better in non-hierarchical organisations and in temporary leadership roles than their male counterparts.

Supervision is another function of front-line management that can be considered in this context. Maddock's (1999) research study found that, despite their contrary intentions, women managers' supervision practice effectively reinforced blame cultures through gagging clauses in their employment contracts. Presumably, Maddock means by this that the clauses effectively prevented supervisors from whistle-blowing on organisational failures, resulting in the continuing pathologisation of individual practice.

Finally, Hewlett (2002) produced research which found that female managers are more likely to live alone without emotional and family support than their male counterparts. Hewlett's research also suggests that the management styles of some women might be affected by these external circumstances, in some cases driving them further into their jobs.

Leadership

French and Raven (1959) argued that the basis of leadership has changed through history, from coercion to legitimacy, to expertise and finally to charisma. In these terms, 'expertise' probably provides the basis for the leadership role of most team leaders and senior practitioners in social work; the shift from legitimacy to expertise is a useful description of the self-image of graduate managers. Although French and Raven's (1959) analysis is now dated and may not be absolutely precise historically, there is evidence of a tendency towards the recruitment of charismatic, inspiring leaders to senior positions. In some areas these are media figures, in keeping with the 'culture of celebrity' detected in Western societies in recent years (Marshall, 2006); for example, Imran Khan and Patrick Stewart have both been appointed to executive positions in universities in recent years. But we do not really know how charismatic leadership works. Shamir et al (1993) suggest that charismatic leaders engage the self-concept of the follower in the mission articulated by the leader, and this has motivational consequences far beyond material reward.

Sometimes team leaders or residential home managers are not considered 'legitimate' or 'expert' in French and Raven's terms and may need to use other approaches such as coercion or reward, or work hard to be likeable. Coercion, however, does not make for a positive working environment and can result in increased staff turnover.

Management in social services

There has arguably been a sea-change in the way that managers are perceived in public services. Far from being the 'folk heroes' identified by Mintzberg in 1973, public sector managers are now widely viewed with scepticism and are occasionally vilified in the media (recently for example in relation to the case of Baby Peter Connelly). Partly, the public sector managerialist revolution of the 1980s, which moved public service managers away from a philosophy of 'wise administration' (Simon, 1945) in the quest for value for money, can be seen as having increased scrutiny of public sector management performance. Drucker's (1989) management by objectives (see **Chapter Nine**), which was always intended to be a philosophy of manager self-development rather than a recipe for public sector responsiveness to need, was echoed in a series of reorganisations, in some cases making each successive reorganisation more difficult to implement than the last, whatever its particular merits (Harris, 1998). Overall, then, these changes in how managers are evaluated may mean that the distinction between autocratic and empowering management styles is of renewed importance in social services.

Writers on social work leadership and management have likewise been critical of the 'mythological' change-leader and cool decision-maker popularised in some organisational behaviour literature (Hughes and Waring, 2007), and in some areas of the related (and fascinating) American genre of management 'guru' literature (Kennedy, 2002). For example, decisions not made (or those which are made by the avoidance of making a decision), appear to be on the rise in the management of social services at the present time, if anecdotal evidence will be allowed on this point.

In the 1990s, many local authority social services departments tried expanding the span of control of budget-holding second-level managers ('service managers'), while removing team leaders ('senior social workers'), with various arrangements for team self-management such as support by senior practitioners. Anecdotal evidence suggests that some authorities have subsequently re-introduced team leaders. There has been, and is still, some confusion of 'leader' and 'senior' roles in teams, to say nothing of the long-standing debate about the role of unqualified workers in teams. Cockburn (1990) interviewed social work team leaders and team managers over twenty years ago and found similar confusion about roles then, which supports the view that restructuring social work organisations has not yet resolved issues of front-line management decisively. It remains to be seen if the Social Work Task Force recommendations for defined training for front-line managers in social work will move things forward.

Overall, if social work Key Roles show a tendency to converge with a model of distributed management, social work values can be seen to be not so much a running critique of the new public management, with its focus upon targets, performance, and budgets (Petrie, 2010), as a collection of cues for how-to-do front-line social work management (Webster, 2010). Empowering front-line practitioners by rotating some management tasks, recognising and respecting their skills and decision-making expertise, acknowledging the cultural milieu in which they work, supporting the sometimes spiritual motivation of practitioners and, by rewarding and valuing them, maintaining workers' self-esteem can all be seen as extensions of the social work core values into the practice of front-line management.

Further on this point, there is a rich literature, emanating from the workers' cooperative movement, the women's movement, from international development capacity building and from elsewhere, on the value of training all staff to be managers (Randall and Southgate, 1980; Ianello, 1992; Manz, 1993; Lee, 2001; Skinner, 2006). This, also, accords with the professional social work value of empowerment and fits with the contemporary structure of distributed management in social services organisations.

In contrast, Hughes and Waring (2007) have observed that the 'hyper-bureaucracy' of current social work practice tends to disempower the social worker by filling working time with paperwork-driven tasks, and this may have a countervailing effect to the trends referred to above. Hughes and Waring suggest negotiating a workload management formula to equalise casework burdens (see also Stevens, 2008), although it is not altogether clear how this could break the cycle of stress and sick leave as they intend, if the result is a back-up of unallocated or 'unopened' cases. Better support and supervision can alleviate stress (Jones and Munro, 2005; Hawkins and Shohet, 2000), but if service quality is to be maintained in the face of increasing workloads either more workers are needed, eligibility criteria for services must become narrower or some other expedient found. Devolving responsibility further to lower-paid workers may appear to be an option in the short run, but training requirements might well prove costly in the medium term.

Participation and empowerment

Savage (1990, 1996) considered the impact of IT on 'steep hierarchies' within organisations and concluded that 'knowledge networking' facilitated by IT was antithetical to such hierarchies, fostering instead participatory decision-making in management. This supports the picture we have of emerging 'open teams' that are outward looking, although there may be some evidence of gender differences in networking. While Savage was perhaps primarily concerned with networking in the private sector, Brown-Graham and Morgan (2007) note its importance in local government service management; and there may be a gendered dimension to this. Hughes and Waring (2007), commenting primarily upon the Australian situation, found more participative decision-making in social services organisations, with networking facilitating service user involvement and more participative management. Yet we may question the extent to which this has happened in British social services organisations, despite legislative change. Participative decision making and democratic management, despite IT support (Harlow and Webb, 2003), do not appear to resemble the Australian experience. Empowering practices, such as the employment of service users at all levels of the organisation, is a model found in women's refuges (Lee, 2001) and a few other organisational settings, but comparatively rarely in mainstream social services.

Conclusion

When asked if there are identifiable traits of social work management we are likely to give a clear description of the kind of manager that we would *not* like to work for. We are then forced to acknowledge that, much of the time, we are actually going to be self-managing anyway, albeit within the support of self-managing teams. Yet, if the current social work and social care Code of Practice requires that we are working for the service user rather than a manager *per se*, the question becomes that of which accountability structure best facilitates this. In short, we do not really escape the search to identify an optimum management environment for social work.

Perhaps the reality in social services is one of policy short termism, accompanied by hyper-bureaucracy, with distributed yet largely disempowered management performing the functions of policy interpretation (Lipsky, 1980), change implementation, information dissemination and gathering, equal opportunities enforcement and tracking of customer need. Indeed, to what extent is the 'empowered' social worker really just 'encumbered' (Grey, 2007)? As we saw in **Chapter Five** on teamwork, this idea fits with the outward-looking, networking, liaising team structure of contemporary social services organisations. Distributed, devolved management functions appear to be accompanied by little real power, belying in this respect the incipient 'masculinisation' of social work detected by Harlow (2000) a decade ago.

In terms of the management function of leadership, it was noted that potentially any employee might exercise this in appropriate circumstances, and that leadership training may intrinsically be a good thing. Buchanan (2003) researched change leadership in a hospital setting, and found that the responsibility for driving change was frequently distributed to nurse 'champions' (Peters, 1987) on the front line; there is similar practice in social work settings. Buchanan (2003) suggested that there could be greater opportunities for women's career development in these settings as a result, but also noted the potential for colleague animosity, and the difficulty of slipping back into a 'normal' professional role after experiencing the organisation in a broader way. Moreover, the roles of champions or change agents tend to be fluid, creating stress, as does being an agent for several different 'stakeholder' interests simultaneously, trying to function normally while implementing change, carrying a heavy workload, and appearing credible to colleagues. Yet front-line change leaders also described the work positively (Buchanan, 2003).

Ideas such as motivational engagement are familiar processes to social workers and to many front-line workers in social care. The person we would rather work for, then, is either the service user (the ethical answer) or the manager who most completely facilitates this relationship.

▶KEY LEARNING POINTS

- Social work roles include a significant degree of self-management and the devolution of many former management functions
- Gender differences in management style are of particular significance to social work
- The core values of social work can be used to inform management practice
- Leadership roles are often based on expertise or personality
- Changes to the basis of leadership or the style of management have significant consequences for staff, for the service unit and in turn for the service user

▶EXERCISE: WHAT MAKES A GOOD MANAGER?

Do this exercise in pairs.

Individually spend about ten minutes listing the characteristics of a manager you found it hard to work with, then repeat the exercise for a manager you enjoyed working with.

Compare experiences with your partner, looking for common features, before attempting to answer the following questions.

Which of the characteristics you have listed related to your managers' practical skills such as decision making, communication and problem solving?

Which characteristics related to their use of self?

CHAPTER NINE

Management strategies: do the costs outweigh the gains?

What you will learn in this chapter

- History of management by objectives
- The advantages and disadvantages of management by objectives approaches in social work
- The impact of total quality management

Introduction

In **Chapter Four**, we looked at decision making, and in particular at the effects of the organisation upon individual decision making. We found that, amongst other organisational influences, managerial strategy could be a force that might impede or facilitate individual decision making. In this chapter, we will look more closely into managerial strategy and management by objectives (MBO) in particular.

What is management by objectives? In a mainstream British management textbook of the 1970s, Cowling and Stanworth (1977) asserted that MBO was 'simply good management' (1977, p 187). It was also considered to be a powerful organisational change agent (see **Chapter Eleven**), if implemented properly.

History of management by objectives

If scientific management can be said to have begun towards the end of the nineteenth century, in the period following the Second World War its characteristic form was that of MBO. Odiorne (1965) identified a series of stages in twentieth-century management strategy:

- hire-and fire between the wars;
- human relations during wartime skill shortages;
- pressured human relations during post-war competition; and
- MBO in the emerging period of consumerism.

The autocratic, hierarchic management found in the giant conglomerates of the 1920s was seen to encourage clock-watching, place-hunting, atrophy and product stultification. Moreover, promotion-as-reward was seen to create a culture of movement rather than of achievement. However, the management strategies adopted by Henry Ford and by General Motors from the 1930s implemented management principles of individual responsibility, involvement in labour relations and contribution planning and knowledge-based strategy: 'Arbitrary orders have been replaced by performance standards based on objectives and measurements' (Drucker, 1989, p 115). These were seen to have been successful strategies and to have demonstrated their superiority over the types of routine administrative management problem solving (Mintzberg, 1973) that preceded them.

It seems likely that the typical form taken by scientific management in the Western European social services organisations of the post-war period was also MBO, even if in practice that eventually came to mean one of a number of hybrids, including total quality management (see below) and the learning organisation (see **Chapter Seven**). The Viennese intellectual Peter Drucker is usually credited with being the first to identify the MBO approach in his book *The Practice of Management* (1955).

Drucker himself claimed that he was merely describing a system in use in the American car industry just after the Second World War. Moreover, he appears to have believed that the system emerged to accompany the smaller units of production which followed the wave of business mergers occurring in Britain, the US and Western Europe around 1920. Drucker viewed MBO as a way of managing business organisations at a certain point in their growth cycle.

Peter Drucker

It is also interesting to note that Drucker fled to London before the outbreak of the Second World War, and his writings from 1939 onwards can perhaps be seen partly as a commentary upon the Third Reich. As he remarks in *The practice of management*, 'There is nothing so useless as doing efficiently what should not be done at all' (Drucker, 1955, p 27). There is a notable similarity between Drucker's work and Whyte's (1956) *Organisation man*, insofar as both writers appear to desire a halt to the proliferation of go-with-the-crowd functionaries.

Drucker's remark also provides us with a good starting point for an outline of MBO: the manager must not simply administrate or be good at her job; her job must have genuine objectives derived from the objectives of the business or organisation as a whole, and her performance as a manager must be measured by her achievement of these, with payment according to the achievement of those objectives. Incidentally, Drucker was clear that first-line supervisors are included in this view of management (Drucker, 1989), and this is something to be considered later when we examine 'distributed' models of management. Because there is a focus upon self-setting of goals, MBO can also be seen as a philosophy of manager self-development, although it is quite different from schemes such as job rotation which formulate personal development in terms of job enrichment. It is interesting to consider the parallel development of American psychology in the mid-1950s, for at this time work psychologists were bringing in 'sensitivity training' for managers, and the ideas of 'Third Force' psychology (including, for example, self actualisation), were emerging (Fast, 1970).

The application of MBO to social work

MBO was adopted by public and voluntary organisations in the late 1970s in North America, in response to calls for value for money in public services. Following the perceived failure of the War On Poverty initiatives of the preceding decade, and a tightening business and fiscal environment following the oil crisis in 1973, public spending on social programmes came under increasingly sceptical review as the 1970s turned to the market liberalism of the 1980s.

MBO was adopted in Britain for similar reasons from the 1980s, marking a shift from intuitive administration to precise, pre-planned management. It is interesting to note, however, that MBO was tried out in the upper management of the British civil service in the late 1960s, and recommended for wider adoption (Chapman and Greenaway, 1980). Obstacles to implementation, such as the absence of profit motive, the different basis of civil service statistics and the devolving tendency of MBO, were noted. Despite the recommendation, the British civil service went on to adopt methods which were more reminiscent of Mayo (1933; and see **Chapter Two**) than characteristic of Drucker, with older methods of performance appraisal and job rotation in evidence in the lower rungs of the civil service in the 1970s.

Advantages of MBO in social work

One of the salient features of the civil service-type bureaucracy found in public services in the 1970s was the relative absence of overt statements of purpose. In the civil service, a standard portrait of Queen Elizabeth II supplied an idealised figurehead, and the Oath of Office perhaps supplied a sense of organisational identity if one were needed. Yet a clearly determined mission arguably leads to better team working and greater effectiveness; one pitfall of losing sight of the overall mission, sometimes observed in public services, is the tendency for means to become ends in themselves. When this happens, public servants become preoccupied with their rules and lose sight of the goals of the service (Merton, 1940). There are a number of possible explanations of this: Kanter (1977) suggested that a combination of detailed regulations coupled with little real power tends to produce a syndrome of behaviours, of which this is a part. Consider, in this light, the once common complaint of social workers that social security clerks were in danger of losing sight of human need in the labyrinth of their eligibility rules.

It was not until the new managerialism of the 1980s that mission statements gained widespread currency in public services. Together with the systematic identification of employee strengths and weaknesses, this approach potentially (if not always in practice) clarified expectations and improved motivation. Scientific planning, faster feedback and better management information went alongside better staff development in managing what Drucker (1969) came to refer to as the 'knowledge workers' of the public services.

Raider (1976) suggests that because of professional autonomy, diffused responsibility and the compromise nature of missions with service users, MBO must be adapted for use in social work organisations, but it can, nonetheless, be used. Raider also suggests using it primarily for planning and communication (with adequate resources), since outcomes such as case closures cannot be given targets.

Criticisms of MBO in social work

There have been, almost from the outset, dissatisfactions with MBO, as the civil service example shows. It takes at least three MBO cycles or years to implement, and five to settle down – a lead-in time that can cause frustration and disappointment. Also, measuring attainment of objectives can be difficult in social work organisations, as can isolating the intervention and attributing accountability. Related to this is the contended nature of theories underpinning change in social work. MBO requires stability, so if the agency's annual budget is uncertain, it probably is not a good candidate; new budgets require new objectives. If the service user group is subject to change, this also makes MBO difficult, as does frequent changes of staff, especially administrative staff. It has been noted that cycles of organisational change tend to get progressively shorter and shorter, eventually reducing to less than 18 months, and this may inhibit MBO schemes. Competing programmes by different supervisors with different objectives (a situation when there are too many managers) may make MBO unworkable.

There is also a high cost to implement MBO, since every aspect of the organisation must be changed, and there are high ongoing costs, chiefly in employee time for reporting purposes and for information feedback. Annual review of organisational objectives and individual goals is hugely expensive of time: 'People often feel that the time spent on paperwork could be better spent on the job itself' (Raider, 1975).

An obvious objection to MBO is that, unlike a commercial enterprise, the function of social services is not to expand its services and increase the number of customers. Finally, there is no research demonstrating that MBO *does* improve productivity or job satisfaction. Research shows that although staff performance appraisal, motivation, planning and communication improve, job satisfaction returns to the former level after 20 months.

Total quality management

Total quality management (TQM) was originally a business-edge strategy of the 1980s (an outcome of the leaner-tougher-smarter days of 1970s post-oil crisis America; Oakland, 2000), and came to British social services with the new managerialism of the same decade. In the explosion of TQM publishing in the early 1990s, there was a TQM text for almost every application, from community colleges to catering, healthcare to residential management. Although Oakland (2000) insists that TQM was the common property of management gurus in the 1980s, he describes how he took the idea from the chemical process industry in which he worked. Each worker in the process identifies the outcome or objective

Figure 9.1: Model of Total Quality Management

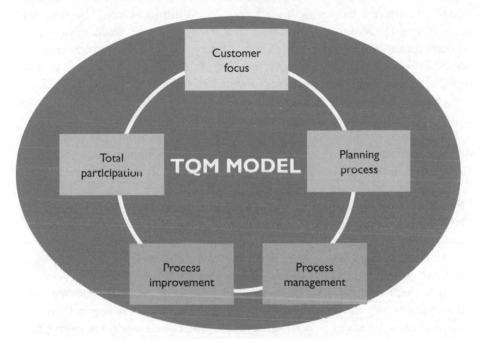

of his particular stage and applies the cycle of evaluate, plan, do, check and amend. Coulshed et al (2006) have argued that the TQM initiative in social services in the 1990s was essentially a culture-change event rather than simply an organisational change (see **Chapter Eleven**); one that made every care manager a TQM manager. According to Oakland (2000), TQM is an approach to quality assurance in organisations that resists 'add-on' application, because every employee is encouraged to engage in continuous innovation to improve the organisation. Whenever we see a customer care helpline number or web address on paperwork, or a 'how's my driving?' message on social services transport, we may be brushing with TQM. If you have spotted job satisfaction surveys coming your way or have heard the words 'benchmarking' and 'world class', you may well have been 'TQMed'. It is possible to see initiatives such as the Department of Health's Quality Protects programme, launched in 1998 to support local authorities in improving their services to children, as a version of TQM (Coulshed et al, 2006).

The results of TQM may not always be entirely satisfactory and effective implementation is not guaranteed (Victor et al, 2000). Obstacles may include poor leadership, under-resourcing, lack of training, absence of consensus over organisational goals and cultural resistance. Since these problems also bedevil other organisational change strategies, they will be discussed in **Chapter Eleven** on organisational change. One of the problems peculiar to TQM appears to be the difficulty of simultaneously delivering a service to the client, on one hand, and thinking about how to improve it, on the other. In particular, Victor et al (2000) contend that organisations in which employees stare off into space in the middle of routine activities are less effective TQM implementers. The argument seems homologous to that around reflective practice in social work, in as much as workers appear to proceed most effectively when they switch between reflective and active modes. At the same time, the idea of customer and supplier working together seems an obvious one to social workers. Perhaps the most difficult doubt to shake is that this was a strategy that worked very well in the chemical process industry, but may not necessarily be as useful in social work.

The practice example below illustrates the way in which TQM can develop into an organisational culture (see **Chapter Six**) in which the adaptation and circumvention of targets becomes institutionalised (McIver, 1991).

Practice example: quality measures and targets

Mr Krazuny, a partially sighted amputee who uses a wheelchair, was accompanied by his social worker on a visit to the outpatients department of the local hospital for tests. The local Hospital Trust published waiting time targets and the social worker correspondingly planned for a total trip time of two hours. Shortly after arrival a nurse ticked Mr Krazuny's name on a list. The social worker then waited nearly two hours before her client was seen. Upon later making a complaint to the Hospital Trust she received an apology but was told that the Trust undertook that a nurse would see the patient within twenty minutes and that this target had been met.

Reflective point

What objectives are driving the targets in this example? Can you think of ways in which this target could have been helpful to the service recipient? Are there any general strategies for working with the TQM cultures of public service organisations?

Conclusion

It is clear that if MBO methods are to be implemented successfully in social work settings, a minimum three-year lead-in is necessary, with the underwriting of staff continuity and long-term budgets and plans. Recent local authority moves in this direction include bursaries, post-qualifying career development and the extension of the personal development plan approach to front-line workers in social services.

However, the older warnings about MBO continue to ring true: as Cowling and Stanworth (1977) observed, any process that involves participatory engagement between managers and other staff will only work when the manager is already on board, creating a sort of 'chicken and egg' situation. Not only will MBO stall in a climate of suspicion, it also requires a relatively well-informed manager, knowledgeable about individual and group behaviour. In short, approaches of this kind work best for well-trained staff in an organisation in which staff relations are already pretty good and will be most effective in organisations in which the practice can be spread throughout the organisation. This is asking a great deal from any local authority setting, even in the twenty-first century, more than 50 years on from the publication of Drucker's (1955) book.

Perhaps one of the most obvious comments that can be made about MBO, and about subsequent variants involving participative goal-setting methods, is that 9-to-5 attitudes to work are not an option in these schemes. Employees can no longer expect to perform their individual task and leave all of the rest of it to their manager. If social workers were ever in any doubt about this, the Key Roles and Capabilities Framework have made it clear once and for all that taking on the goals, values and responsibilities of the organisation in which they operate is an integral part of the job. Further discussion of the consequences of this approach will be included in **Chapter Eleven** on organisational change.

> ▸**KEY LEARNING POINTS**
>
> - Managerial strategies have systematic effects upon social work practice.
> - MBO is a generic strategy, or strategy family, used widely in the public sector.
> - Research on the application of MBO in social work settings points to fairly long lead-in periods and to problems of outcome measurement

> ▸**EXERCISE: PAPER SCULPTURES**
>
> This exercise is known as the 'paper boats', 'paper aeroplanes', or the 'origami' exercise. The class divides into two teams and separates to mutually exclusive areas of the room. Each team operates as a self-contained production unit, setting its own objectives, quality standards, production targets, role specialisation, team identity and motivational methods. Both teams first produce the item – be it a paper boat, plane or origami shape such as a bird – with each worker making individual items for three minutes. The lecturer gathers information from each team and writes output figures in a comparative grid on display. Next, each team produces the item for three minutes using division of labour and defined objectives, with each worker doing one or two folds. Work songs or chants are permitted provided they do not inconvenience students in adjacent classrooms. Piles of scrap paper will be needed and should later be recycled.

CHAPTER TEN

Power and the organisation: who really controls social services?

What you will learn in this chapter

- Organisational theories of power, including Mintzberg's power configurations
- An understanding of hidden power
- Gender dimensions of power and gender stratification
- Practices of power at organisational and individual levels
- Issues of empowerment for service users
- Organisational power in social work

Introduction

At the most abstract level of analysis, power is the capacity to materialise thought, to mobilise resources or to get other people to do things they might not otherwise do. In organisational terms power can be defined as the capacity to produce results consistent with your objectives, so mission statements, management and personal goals, team objectives, customer need and stakeholder interests all intersect with issues around power in organisations (see **Chapter Nine** on management by objectives).

Power and control can also be drivers of organisational change (as will be discussed in **Chapter Eleven**): the two major drivers of organisational change in social services in recent decades have been financial constraints and changing ideas about who should, and who does, control social services.

This chapter will begin by reviewing theories of power from the organisational behaviour literature and considering their relevance to social services organisations. Organisational behaviour theories will be compared and contrasted with social work theories of power. Finally, both bodies of theory will be brought together in an attempt to understand who has power in social services organisations.

Organisational theories of power

Before and during the Second World War, analysis of power in the organisational literature was primarily concerned with rational–economic or 'rational–legal' (Weber, 1947) models of power. In the post-war period a plethora of social–psychological theories of personal and group power conflicted with the existing models, leading to a fragmentary and inconclusive picture. However, from these classic theories Buchanan and Huczynski (2004) distinguish three types of power in organisations:

1. Power as a property of individuals
2. Power as a property of relationships
3. Power as a property of structures.

It is power as a property of relationships that we will consider here.

French and Raven: relational power

Social psychologists John French and Bertram Raven (1959) argued that power is relational, that is depending not on individual qualities but on relationships between people. They identified six bases of relational power:

- Positional power: based on an individual's position within the organisation.
- Referent power: which builds on individual power attributes, such as charaisma and interpersonal skills, which can be used to build loyalty and influence.
- Expert power: based on skills and specialist expertise of the individual.
- Reward power: based on an individual's access to rewards and ability to use those to motivate others.
- Coercive power: use of fear and reprisals to ensure the obedience of others.
- Informational power: based on the use of information which can simply be data of value, but can be exercised through rational argument and persuasion.

Mintzberg: power in organisations

Pluralistic understandings of power (such as Dahl, 1963) recognise that there are many possible loci of power; that power is not located within individuals but within the organisation. In his analysis of power in organisations Mintzberg (1983) attempted to bring together rational and psychological theories to identify typologies of internal organisational power, as well as analysing the players both inside and outside of the organisation who had power. Mintzberg (1983) identified six 'ideal type' internal power configurations of organisations:

1. the Autocracy
2. the Instrument
3. the Closed System

4. the Missionary
5. the Meritocracy
6. the Political Arena.

To a large extent these titles are self-explanatory. The Autocratic power system requires loyalty to the chief executive officer; in social work there are some small voluntary organisations that operate in this way and some small organisations move in and out of this model during times of crisis. The Instrument power system is usually a bureaucracy in the service of a dominant external influencer, which describes local authority social services when they are tightly controlled by external policy dictates or by a tight financial environment. The Closed System describes what happens when the bureaucrats have got the upper hand. An example of this could be the type of civil service ministry lampooned in the 1980s British TV sitcom *Yes Minister,* or depicted in C.P. Snow's (2000) novel of elite academic management *The masters.*

In the Missionary ideal type of organisational power system, individuals anywhere in the organisation draw power from the ideological goals of the organisation; Mintzberg (1983) suggested that Alcoholics Anonymous and the Irish Republican Army were examples of this type of power configuration in an organisation. Here, the aims of the organisation may be imposed upon the wider society. Of the remaining two types of internal power configuration, the Meritocracy draws its power from the expertise of its core professional staff. Different professional groups may argue over resources and territory and overlook overall organisational aims in doing so, but wield common power in relation to those external to the organisation. Examples of this are public health service organisations and social work in hospital settings. Finally, the Political Arena organisational power configuration is one in which conflict is routine: imagine a sort of House of Commons with party infighting and factions. Mintzberg (1983) may have been thinking of military organisations in which rivalry is all but institutionalised, but this ideal type could also describe some welfare conglomerates. A local authority or a government ministry may comprise several service units and the dissolution of a powerful quango (a quasi-autonomous non-governmental organisation) may precipitate a free-for-all of jostling for position between the remaining units. A similar situation may arise between the subsidiaries of a large corporation when one is sold off or dissolved. Organisations can move between these different internal power configurations, depending upon a variety of factors.

Lukes: hidden power

Lukes (1974) takes an 'interactionist' view of power, arguing that the 'unseen' dimensions of power must also be considered. Lukes distinguishes the visible forum of power (for example a Social Services Committee), the hidden forum of power (such as the golf course or club) and the organisation: how decisions are made may not be up for discussion, for example.

For many practical purposes, though, perceived power is real power. For example, if you believe me to be an important person in my organisation, you will take my initial advice to you as a newcomer to the organisation seriously. Later, when you discover that I am a rather marginal organisational player and departmental sideliner, you will perhaps treat me with the moderated respect I probably deserve.

Practice example: the decision-making forum

Jyostna Budwal had been working with Suzanne, a young woman in the looked after system, around problems with her birth father, when Suzanne told her she had heard the community home she was living in was going to close. She felt the home was one of the few relatively stable points in her life and was distressed at the prospect of another move. Jyostna investigated the rumour and found that the home was indeed scheduled for closure. At her client's instigation, after a three-way meeting at the home with one of the elected members of the local council, she arranged for both of them to attend a meeting of a social services sub-committee to present the service users' case for keeping the home open.

The day of the meeting arrived and Jyostna and her client were brought in to the sub-committee. At first Jyostna had difficulty understanding the discussion: the elected members appeared to be engaged in banter about previous administrations, even though she had been assured on admission that the home closure was currently under discussion. Jyostna waited for her client to be invited to present her case and eventually succeeded in getting the attention of the chairperson. Her client spoke for a few moments but almost immediately the bantering exchange between different political factions of the elected members continued.

As they were driving back to the home after the meeting, Suzanne said that it didn't seem as if they were really discussing the fate of the home at all. It was as if the decision had already been made at some other meeting and the meeting was only used for the presentation of political positions.

Gender and power

When mainstream organisational behaviour textbooks do broach the subject of gender and power the issue is usually viewed in terms of positional power within the organisation (Robbins 2001, for example, has a section on sexual harassment in organisations). Thus male supervisor A harasses female supervisee B because of the power he has due to his superior position in a hierarchical organisation. While an acknowledgement of this is undoubtedly useful, status and position are competitive attributes which have been seen by some as distinctively male concerns (Jackson and Carter, 2000). As with other areas of organisational behaviour, the traditional literature views the world from a male perspective; after all, much of the classic research in the discipline was carried out in largely male-managed organisations. However, this narrow view omits the influence of power relations imported into the organisation from the wider society or uncritically accepts them as common knowledge.

Illich (1983) in *Gender* argued that gender power is relational, and is based on a complex relation, pre-existing industrial society, comprising separate but complementary activities. These are seen to have been 'emptied out' in modern organisations, such that men's power within organisations can arise from other sources. Consequently men and women increasingly do the same work, but women may lose self-worth because they are deprived of traditional, relational sources of gender value. Men meanwhile remain super-ordinate but increasingly in conflict with women. It is not clear whether Illich's analysis is good historiography, however. The argument that industrialisation deprives women of value because it disturbs a zero-sum power relation, based upon complementary activities, effectively explains contemporary organisational conflict in terms of a remote past. This implies a permanence to behaviours that may in fact be susceptible to change. Baron and Straus (1987) identify a theory of power in which gender stratification is seen to be maintained by the tacit threat of sexual violence, both within organisations and outside them. The subordination of women within organisations is influenced by events outside of the organisation, even to the level of global events such as wars in which women appear as victims of sexual violence. In a similar way, Buchanan (2003) distinguishes embedded, invisible power in organisations.

Furthermore, the implications of the analysis of the gender dimension to power and oppression raise questions about the mainstream analysis of power in the organisational behaviour literature generally. For example, Grimwood and Popplestone (1992) note that male managers in organisations are more concerned with status and position power than their female counterparts. In this respect, an initial concern (as in Mintzberg's 1973 model) is that there is an implicit pluralist ('competing interest groups') model of power. This model views the operation of power as being something akin to that in a caricatured House of Representatives: the group that shouts loudest wins the day. The potential weakness of such a model is that, in an unsophisticated form, it can tacitly assume the existence of a level playing field, whereas the reality is that some parties are likely to be in a minority or oppressed position. Furthermore, this may have little to do with 'interests' as such and more to do with contingent attributes such as age or gender.

Practices of power

Foucault: disciplinary power of the organisation

In his classic work *Discipline and punish* Foucault (1975) outlined a 'disciplinary' type of power which pervades every aspect of organisations: he referred to bio-power, which operates by distinguishing the normal from the abnormal. The organisation influences power though its official 'discourse', establishing the range of the normal and thereby defining the roles and actions of the individual employee. This approach is useful because it offers an explanation of why staff in an organisation continue to work without being continually overlooked. The self-management of social workers would therefore not imply individual power and control.

The 'disciplinary' practices of the organisation might include lots of small repetitive processes, such as barrier-entry to car parks, log-ins and key card entry, ID use, mileage recording and even determined career paths. The social worker becomes as much a prisoner of the organisation, as the client is of the 'gaze' (Foucault, 1975) of the welfare organisation. It follows that organisational restructuring does not really change the underlying power dynamics.

Individual power tactics

From this logical extremity of the structural view of organisational power, we now turn to the power tactics employed by individuals in organisations.

Classical theories of power, as with classical theories of decision-making, assume a rational and constant individual making consistent choices. In the 1980s, however, more cynical political models became fashionable, sometimes called Machiavellian models (named after Niccolò Machiavelli, the fifteenth-century Italian political philosopher). In this model of 'political' power behaviour, people rarely give the real reason for their actions. Power strategies in this model might include never trusting anyone completely, telling people what they want to hear, using the end to justify the means, and believing that revenge is a valid motive. Research by Kipnis and Schmidt (1980), for example, with several hundred subjects identified the following influencing strategies:

* friendliness;
* reasoning;
* coalition-forming;
* bargaining;
* use of sanctions (behaviourism);
* assertion of higher authority;
* making the other feel important;
* invoking of past favours (the use of a 'favour bank');
* filing a report with a supervisor;
* becoming a nuisance;
* expressing anger;
* blocking the other's actions;
* giving unsatisfactory performance evaluations; and
* ignoring the other or withdrawing friendship.

Sculpture of Niccolò Machiavelli in Florence

Several of these actions, most notably the last two listed here, could constitute bullying, harassment or emotional abuse.

It should be noted that Kipnis and Schmidt (1980) found that gender was not a factor in choosing a strategy of influence, contrary to what has been said elsewhere about the emotional strategies employed by women in counselling and supervision situations, and their (good) reasons for using these strategies (Taylor, 1994).

Buchanan and Huczynski (2004) also found a number of power tactics, including:

- image building;
- use of selective information;
- scapegoating;
- formal alliances;

- networking;
- compromising; and
- rule manipulation.

They also identify the following covert and ruthless tactics:

- undermining of expertise;
- keeping a 'dirt' file;
- coercion;
- playing one person or group off against another;

- undermining opponents with rumours;
- criticising others' plans; and
- the use of others to 'fire bullets'.

Although these are simple lists, they cover a wide range of behaviours. Being able to identify a power strategy or combination of strategies can render the behaviours sharply visible and may provides a basis for reflecting on a colleague's motives and intentions.

External influencing strategies

Adapting his 1979 model of organisational structure (see Figure 1.1 in **Chapter One**), Mintzberg (1983) identified a number of players who can exert influence on organisations, both from the inside and from the outside. In the external influencers, he included clients, partners, as well as government agencies at national and local levels, special interest groups and the general public – all of which are relevant to public service organisations. Mintzberg (1983) also identified eight strategies of influence that can be used by these players (although there are perhaps more). These strategies are:

1. Nationalise it
2. Ignore it
3. Democratise it
4. Regulate it

5. Pressure it
6. Restore it
7. Induce it
8. Trust it.

We might add 'Dissolve it' to this list, since this has been a strategy used to exert power over public organisations recently.

Figure 10.1: Mintzberg's 'cast of players'

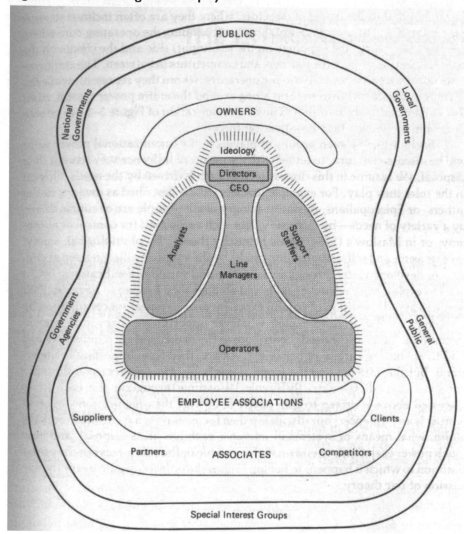

Source: Mintzberg, 1983, p 29.

Reflective point

Think about how these strategies could be operationalised in relation to social services before reading on.

Nationalisation as a strategy for regaining control of a voluntary or private organisation seen to be deficient in social responsibility or in its responsiveness to the needs of its service users, should be familiar to most readers. The drawbacks of this are high cost, staff resistance to change and the relative distance of the 'client' from policy formation and organisational change.

'Ignore it' may be a strategy in some public services but is not an option for failing child protection services for example. Democratisation, in the sense of the inclusion of service users in internal management and change, is a popular strategy at present and has been implemented with some success in Australian social services. If by 'Democratise it' we mean industrial participation (Pateman, 1970), then we must consider how far social workers would be willing, appropriately skilled or have enough free time to participate in the direction and management of social services.

'Regulate it' is a bureaucratic, central government response to unsatisfactory services, but it is only as effective as the willingness of the organisation's front-line workers to cooperate and their interpretation of the policy and procedures of regulation (Lipsky, 1980). 'Pressure it' is a much-used strategy by consumer and service user groups; the success of this approach varies. In public services 'Restore it' refers to reprivatisation. The downside of this is power without the same levels of social responsibility; the upside can be smaller, more responsive organisations and greater diversity of provision. 'Induce it' refers to the provision of incentives to change organisations. The Investors in People scheme is an example of such an incentive scheme that appears to have successfully achieved its objectives. Alternatively, dental Capitation and Quality Scheme Agreements, under which money is received by the dentist for every patient taken, can increase the number of NHS patients, but might mean that individual patients are seen at longer intervals than they were formerly. Finally, 'Trust it' seems to refer to the strategy of allowing corporations to police themselves and one another. Sometimes this works, arguably it has done with corporate care home owners, nursery chains and independent schools (although not everyone would agree with this). Sometimes it does not work quite so well, for example in the banking sector over the past decade.

Theories of power in social work

For several decades the value base of social work has rested on the assumption that power is not primarily interpersonal, or even organisational, but systemic: certain groups and individuals do not have an equal chance to participate in societal opportunities because of their comparatively disempowered, oppressed status in society as a whole (Dominelli, 2002). As noted above, the handling of power in mainstream organisational behaviour literature does not often take these wider societal influences into account, so theories from organisational behaviour must be qualified before they can be applied to social work organisations.

As has been noted in previous chapters, we are dealing, in social work, with predominantly female organisations and we might not expect the dynamics of interpersonal power to be the same in social work as in male-dominated organisations (Grimwood and Popplestone, 1992).

Dressel (1987) argues that power in social work operates one step (hierarchically) back from the front-line, to control the 'messy' emotional labour of women's work and squeeze it into the forms of patriarchal discourse (Opie, 2000). This interpretation is similar in many ways to that offered by Wilson (1996), in terms of which the power of men in organisations rests upon and needs the subordination of women at the bottom of the organisation.

In her later work, Wilson (2004) starts with the assumption that aspects of work in social work organisations are intrinsically oppressive and draws together a number of strands of research focusing on the resistance offered by social care and other workers in these organisations. It might be believed that the type of resistance used by social workers around dissatisfactions in their work (such as caseload size) is dealt with in a largely passive manner, such as the taking of sick leave. However, Wilson suggests that resistance in the caring professions may sometimes be of a more active kind, including controlling (and occasionally abusive) behaviours with service users. This may be an example of a mismatch between public perceptions of women's infinite capacity to care and the reality of poorly paid, long hours of dirty and difficult work (Wilson, 2004).

Power in supervision

Hugman (1991) makes two detailed points in his discussion of power in social work supervision. First, social workers do not, typically, make decisions at the point of service user contact (although emergency duty teams and duty social workers may routinely see exceptions to this). Rather, it is in supervision or in discussion with a senior colleague or line manager that decisions are most often made, or at least ratified. Hugman argues that this is evidence of the clear operation of hierarchical power and the relatively disempowered status of the field social worker. Second,

there is what Hugman (1991) calls 'hierarchical control of knowledge' in social work, and this again is something he takes as clear evidence of power hierarchy and front–line social worker disempowerment. This is conceived to work by the social worker adjusting her casework to fit the known discourse of acceptable knowledge in social work, and the supervisor imposing the discourse firmly upon it (see the discussion of Foucault earlier in this chapter).

Brown and Bourne (1996) identify a number of ways in which gender, race and membership of other oppressed groups can become a target of blocking strategies in supervision. In these instances, the organisation is influenced by the wider society insofar as relations of oppression outside the organisation are reproduced within it by, in this instance, supervision practices. This resonates with the models of gender oppression in organisations examined earlier in this chapter.

Social workers and office politics

Another aspect of the operation of power in social work organisations can be understood as the popular notion of 'office politics'. What are office politics? Explained simply they are the strategies used by employees to exert influence over colleagues. Individuals may involve themselves in office politics for many reasons covered elsewhere in this book: because of the culture of the organisation (see **Chapter Six**), the leadership style of their line manager (see **Chapter Eight**), the structure of the organisation (see **Chapter One**) or changes their organisation may be going through (see **Chapter Eleven**), informal communication (see **Chapter Three**), and individual motivations (see **Chapter Two**). Some organisational cultures, for example, create insecurity and a climate of suspicion, as do some 'loyalty' and autocratic managerial styles or entrenched informal 'grapevine' communication practices. The motivational and promotional practices of the organisation can also push people towards using office politics in informal 'manoeuvring for position', using negative power tactics over colleagues and canvassing support. Many of these power and influencing strategies will be familiar to social workers, and some can border on or actually merge into harassment, bullying and other oppressive activities. This raises the question of how best to respond to or negotiate office politics. There are many books and internet sites offering general guidance on surviving office politics; however, the Code of Practice (GSCC, 2010) for social care workers and employers gives expression to values which, if applied to 'office politics' situations, offer guidelines which are remarkably similar to the advice offered in self-help books and websites. For example, the Code enjoins:

* transparency
* valuing others, and
* appropriate use of supervision.

All three of these aspects of professional conduct in social work are recommended by non-social work advice as behaviours that will help employees to survive office politics.

Service users and empowerment

Lipsky (1980) might argue that the power of social services exists at the point of delivery, that is, at the interface between the client and provider of public services. As far as the client is concerned, the social worker *is* social services and is therefore invested in power. Any attempts to empower the client must therefore happen at this interface and only if the social worker facilitates this.

Since the end of the 1950s, there has been concern that the delivery of social services in 'total' institutions creates a sharp polarisation of powerless service users and potentially all-powerful front-line staff in these organisations (Goffman, 1957; Townsend, 1962). A series of social policy initiatives from the late 1960s sought to empower service users in a number of ways, such as delivering services in the community (that is direct to people's homes, where it was thought they would have more power), marketising services to create more choice for consumers and, more recently, personalising budgets so that service users structured their own services rather than the social worker or manager. Alongside this, a series of policies were developed dealing with the rights of service users (such as legislation recognising the rights of children, carers, people with disabilities and older people), some of them led initially by European human rights legislation. These have also driven organisational change in social services in the direction of further empowering the consumers of social services.

Organisational strategies for empowerment

However, it may be asked how far this combined pressure towards organisational change has in fact put the service user in the driving seat. Although community services were delivered to the service user in her or his own home to empower the service user, such services have a tendency to turn the home into a version of the institutional environment (Hugman, 1991). In some cases, a constant stream of visitors from diverse agencies or service delivery units can be experienced by the service user as an invading force. The service user's home becomes dominated by care plans and records, time sheets, and the paraphernalia of equipment and medication. Care support staff have remarked how the need to provide efficient support sometimes results in a (perhaps intrusive) reorganising of the contents of the home.

Something similar might be said of the marketisation of services and the personalisation of services. Marketisation undoubtedly increased consumer choice, but even the strongest proponents of marketisation of social services have recognised that there were initially (and perhaps still are) 'market failures'. Some areas of provision (such as dementia care, especially for middle-aged people) continue to offer very limited choice. Personalisation, although theoretically replacing service-driven social work with consumer-led, tailored services, has also met with market failures, such as the lack of availability of sufficiently flexible support services for some activities. In short, service user empowerment has fallen considerably below the expectations of these strategies.

Even where a rights-based approach succeeds in making service user consultation and involvement mandatory, there is an observed tendency of professional behaviours such as boundary-making and accountability to operate in a way that sometimes results in the 'othering' of the service user, which in itself can be disempowering and alienating for the service user (Hugman, 1991). The location of the service user within the professional knowledge base and the nature of such professional knowledges is that they can label and objectify the service user (Boss, 1970; Dressel, 1987), even when it is the express intention of the practitioner to avoid this.

Care and control

It is impossible to discuss the effects of the social services organisation upon the power dynamics between social worker and client without considering what Hugman (1991) has referred to as the 'care and control' element in social work. This refers to the aspects of social work in which some restriction of individual freedom may be an outcome of the intervention, including, among other things, the cluster of skills comprised in risk management. The term 'risk management' is contentious: Holt (2004) suggests that it may sometimes mask highly volatile situations with a veneer of 'tameness'. There are clearly some social work situations in which no amount of risk at all is acceptable, but it is arguable that 'risk management' approaches may lead to a broader range of potential strategies than 'care and control', which represents an either/or strategy.

Empowering structures and processes

Organisational structures and processes can also inhibit a minimally disempowering and maximally cooperative engagement with service users, tilting the balance of power away from the service user. Examples of such structures would be communication-inhibiting organisations – such as Grey's 'steep hierarchies', that restrict horizontal communication between departments and agencies, enclosing social workers in inward-looking teams (Grey, 2007). Organisational cultures (see **Chapter Six**) that inhibit professional supervision and impede the making of good-quality decisions can also disempower service users. Also, despite the primary focus of this book upon the impact of the organisation, the influence of wider society, with which the organisation 'traffics' culturally, should not be ignored. Sharland (2006) has noted, for example, that wider cultural understandings about appropriate risk-taking and risk-making for young people can influence social work decisions, suggesting that this is another aspect about which social workers need to be doubly vigilant in their reflection. Sharland draws attention to the 'moral panic' dimensions of societal culture, within which conceptions of risk can occasionally become distorted.

Conclusion

In this chapter, models of organisational power and control were examined. First, the traditional models of power outlined in organisational behaviour texts have been considered, including a discussion of the limits of traditional models with regard to gender and other forms of oppression. Then the rights-based and consumer empowerment model implicit in much social work writing was very briefly outlined. Some of the weaknesses of both models were identified: the gender bias of the organisational behaviour model, and the market failures and 'othering' tendency of the consumer empowerment and rights-based approach. But are these models mutually exclusive? Possibly not.

The organisational behaviour model of power describes fairly well the behaviour of relatively empowered individuals in organisational settings for two reasons. First, these individuals tend to be men; and second, they tend to occupy the better-paid and more secure career-structured positions in an organisation, where the orientation of the individual is therefore more likely to be concerned with progression. The rights-based approach, by contrast, better describes the power experiences of many clients and of workers in the lower-paid, insecure, temporary or part-time jobs in the organisation. These workers (and clients) are often female and relatively powerless; if they are able to wield any power at all, it tends to be as part of an identity 'collectivity'. This is not to say that rights-based power does not operate among workers who hold greater power (or status), or that the interpersonal power strategies described in the organisational behaviour literature are not used by clients, carers and care workers. It does and they are. It is rather that, like consumer power, these different power strategies are used in different ways, to different ends, and with different results.

Finally, Buchanan (2003) suggests that although Machiavellianism has always been around, the economic conditions of the late twentieth century were especially conducive to it. Partly, this is because managers no longer just tinker with efficiency, but constantly restructure the whole organisation. Despite explicit initiatives to the contrary, the effect is that the model of shared organisational goals and individual consistency is increasingly abandoned; there is increased job insecurity and career paths disappear. People change their jobs and organisations more often and become more aware of the temporary, local nature of goals and missions. One result is that they retreat into their own individual, unique life-plan. Grand narratives thus become less useful for explaining what is happening in organisations, and Buchanan identifies a 'culture of complaint' as one symptom of this.

So who really controls social services? There is a strong and popular argument that service users *ought* to control them, and a similar consensus that in practice they do not. Some take the view that in practice the workers who deliver front-line services in effect *are* social services, to the service user at least, a view which might fit the personal if not the professional aspirations of some social workers, but one which most practitioners would recognise as inaccurate. Relatively few writers since Drucker (1955) have even suggested that front-line managers control anything strategically speaking and the trend of organisational behaviour literature in recent years seems to be that the lower levels of management may do more harm than good if they attempt to control teams which might otherwise be self-managing (see **Chapter Eight**). So, does the executive committee control social services, or are they simply the tool of the elected members? Or are they controlled by the ubiquitous local authority circular from central government, and therefore by the policy and planning department? The attempts of Dahl (1963) and others to locate power in the decision-making process were, as we saw, snared in assumptions about the nature of decision making itself. The decision-making approach is the commonsense, layperson's approach to answering the question of who controls social services and has much to recommend it. The pluralist model offered by Mintzberg (1983) was criticised for missing out the key dimension of systemic distortions of power but it probably provides the best overall description of observable behaviour in controlling social services: a plethora of pressure groups and interest groups, such as charities, service user groups, unions, professional associations and business interests lobby and pressure the decision process, which, even if the executive acts by avoiding decision, in the end gives us the service we subsequently receive, the one that is available within the resources. If that last sentence looks suspiciously close to 'the accountants, ultimately, control social services', it is probably a good point at which to halt the chapter before we transgress into welfare economics, which is beyond the scope of this book.

▶KEY LEARNING POINTS

- Theories of power in the organisational behaviour literature tend to reflect research on male managers in large American corporations, and often enshrine managerial control and efficiency values
- Gender and other power differentials in the wider society may be imported into social work organisations, affecting working conditions and service delivery
- Practices of power can include a wide range of behaviours, including covert or bullying tactics
- Social work conceptions of power often have an emancipatory purpose, which is written into the core values of the profession
- Rights-based approaches will not always offer service users power in public services

CHAPTER ELEVEN

Organisational change: do welfare organisations resist change?

What you will learn in this chapter

- What organisational change is and why organisations change
- Approaches to managing change in organisational contexts
- The impact of change on the individual
- Politics and history of organisational change in social work
- Understanding of what organisational change means for contemporary social work, including the impact of gender

Introduction

Some social workers and service users, many of whom have significant organisational experience, believe that the social work organisation needs a good shake up, while others feel that social work needs time to adjust to past upheavals. Organisational change in social work might be new ways of planning and delivering services that involve service users. The picture presented of changes to private sector business organisations over the last few decades (for example, Kanter, 1994; Watson, 1995) can be applied to welfare agencies too, whether in the private, voluntary or statutory sectors, suggesting a blurring of distinctions and some convergence of organisational structure. There are several ways of viewing recent changes in social work organisations. This chapter aims to connect with experiences of organisational change, and at the same time to explore whether there are features of welfare organisations that render them especially resistant to organisational change.

The chapter will also consider whether organisational change in social services has latent, unintentional or even covert functions which are more or less important than the ostensible, manifest functions of such change. In short a critical attitude towards theories of organisational change will be adopted.

Coulshed et al (2006) drew freely upon organisational theory, from Weber's (1964) theory of bureaucracy (see **Chapter One**) to Senge's (1990) use of systems theory, in their analysis of management in social work. We intend to draw upon some of the same sources here, but with some key differences. First, we are less concerned about the problems posed for management by organisational change than we are about the social worker's experience of and response to such change. Second, gender will form a more critical standpoint from which to view mainstream organisational theory than it perhaps could for Coulshed et al (2006) given the limited space available to them. Third, we will argue that social work has from its origins in the nineteenth century been reciprocally informed by organisational theory.

Models of organisational change

Burke (2002) takes the view that organisations change all of the time, typically in response to changes in the environment in which they operate. Yet organisations can get out of step with their environment or fall behind and require strategic, managed change to bring them back in line. This is in essence an organic, equilibrium model of organisational change, based upon the biological or evolutionary metaphor of species adaptation to habitat. There are other models, based for example on the views that organisational change is a strategy for tightening or reasserting control of the workforce, or for managerial career advancement, or of continuous change designed to wrong-foot competitor organisations to gain a competitive edge in a tight market (Peters, 1987). Strategic change is transformative change which is thrust upon the organisation by changes in the external environment, which, in the case of social services, could be demographic change, for example.

Scientific management theory from Taylor onwards (see **Chapter One**) can also be seen as concerned with organisational change. If we think of the analysis of organisational culture, the study of motivation, the study of management and attempts to improve communication and decision making as aspects of organisational change (Grey, 2007), organisational change can be seen as the nub of the whole discipline of organisational behaviour. This view, although a very persuasive one, is not necessarily shared by all theorists; some argue that it is the relatively enduring and universal features of organisations that constitute the proper subject of the study of organisational behaviour, such as predictable patterns of interaction, group behaviour and individual motivation (Barnard, 1948).

Managing change

Burke (2002) noted that organisational change can be seen as taking place at three levels: the individual level; the team level; and the organisational level. Change strategies usually target each of these levels separately.

So, for example, at the individual level the organisation might offer training courses, such as the individual sensitivity training for managers in large corporations that appeared in post-war North America. This was intended to increase individual managers' awareness of their influence and behaviour (Fast, 1970) and thereby shift organisational culture.

At the team level, teambuilding days might be introduced to re-orient teams. At the organisational level, roadshows and briefing sessions might be used to communicate a new vision and mission statement.

Figure 11.1: Kotter's eight-step model of organisational change

Identify a crisis
↓
Form a guiding coalition or steering group
↓
Create a vision
↓
Communicate the vision
↓
Empower people to act on the vision
↓
Create short-term wins
↓
Consolidate
↓
Institutionalise

Kotter and Schlesinger (1979) developed an eight-step model of managing organisational change (see Figure 11.1). Relating this to social work, some of the steps could be:

- Identify a crisis: for example the increased needs of an ageing population, or a financial squeeze.
- Form a guiding coalition or steering group, perhaps with elected members.
- Create a vision, community care for example.
- Communicate the vision, perhaps with internal briefings and roadshows.
- Empower people to act on the vision, perhaps by appointing champions.
- Create short-term wins, for example saving homes from closure by reassignment, preventing redundancies.
- Consolidate: by investing in new signs, letterhead and stationery, for example.
- Institutionalise, by bringing in a rolling programme of training, new recruitment procedures, job descriptions and induction programmes.

One criticism of this type of otherwise very useful and detailed model of organisational change is that it ignores organisational history and context. Staff teams have histories and these can affect organisational change in unpredictable and sometimes highly resistant ways. The model also ignores 'social loafing' (the tendency for team members to slow down when working in groups on new tasks), which has serious consequences for efficiency.

Change leadership

Buchanan (2003) and others have found a tendency for change initiatives to be abandoned as managers move on. Change leadership is therefore considered a crucial dimension of managing organisational change (Burke, 2002), and 'change agents' and 'champions' will be identified early on.

Moreover, change in organisational culture, which is usually considered the most important change, is almost never tackled head-on. Instead, behaviour change is attempted, with the expectation that culture change will eventually follow, perhaps after a period of five years or more. Burke is also an adherent of the 'tipping point' model of change, according to which change reaches a sort of critical mass of, say, 150 people behaving in changed ways, after which the rest of the organisation changes spontaneously. Those with social services experience may perhaps recognise this phenomenon.

Kanter (1994) argued for a sort of 'organisational free trade' theory of strategic change: good change leaders demonstrate openness to other organisations' and departments' practices and to diverse ideas. She calls this an 'integrationist' approach and states that integrationists 'think outside the box'. In social services, this kind of approach could be the basis for hot-desking, having files on wheels, spending a half-day with a GP practice, block contracts or nurses making placements in community care settings. The integrationist approach would include anything that is not bureaucratic and is non-compartmentalising, organisationally speaking: 'segmentalist', in Kanter's terms. Peters (1987) suggested 'champions' as change-leading front-line workers and this approach has been used in the NHS and to a lesser extent in social services.

Personal responses to change

Buchanan (2003) reports finding initiative fatigue among the staff studied in his research. Loss theory (Kubler-Ross, 1969) can be usefully used to explain some of the effects of change on the individual. The grief stages of denial, anger, bargaining, depression and acceptance can all be detected in responses to some types of change. This model does fit home closures and colleague reassignment, for example, but not necessarily structural change.

Burke (2002) recognises several different types of resistance to organisational change: for example, 'ignore it and it will go away', 'we've seen it all before', apathy and taking refuge in nostalgia. An alternative argument is that change is useful because it raises pressure and produces more work from people, or major change implementation may provide new opportunities and be good for a manager's career (Buchanan, 2003).

Kotter and Schlesinger (1979) identified strategies for overcoming resistance to change:

- Training: for example knowledge 'cascades' and certificates of achievement
- Participation: for example roadshows
- Support: for example mentoring
- Negotiation: including union involvement

- Co-optation: promotion of perceived 'difficult' staff
- Coercion: "It's this or redundancies".

Is painless organisational change possible?

Abrahamson (2000) argues that it is possible to make organisation change painless. He suggests only tinkering with existing structures, rather than implementing recurrent sweeping changes which generate cynicism and burnout: 'see good practice and copy it' might be an example of such an approach in social services, or 'Kludging', which is the implementation of big change, but at the periphery, for example adding a new role, like that of Childhood Obesity Officer. Abrahamson also recommends appointing a 'Chief Memory Officer' who remembers 'the last time this was tried, and what went wrong'.

The darker side of organisational change

Victor and Stephens (1994), Kakabadse et al (2005) and others have argued that the proliferation of new organisational forms since the 1970s has had a 'dark side' of negative consequences. Post-bureaucratic, de-layered (and re-layered), information-rich, networked and ICT-outsourced organisations are seen to have demanded more from employees and placed strains upon society.

In his book *Managers not MBAs* (2004) Mintzberg argues that each MBA 'fad', from Drucker's *Practice of management* (1955) to Peters and Waterman's *In search of excellence* (1982), Kanter's employee empowerment in *The change masters* (1985) and Hamel and Prahalad's *Core competencies* (1990), has stacked up a backlog of organisational change, rather than automatically heralding efficiency. A backlash against fads followed (Johnson, 2010).

However, Collins (2000) points out that although academics criticise management fads they do not engage with management directly, unlike the consultants implementing the strategies and changes.

Changing bureaucracy

There have been a number of critics of the inward-looking tendencies of bureaucracies: for example, Belbin (1996) argues that bureaucracy must go because it adapts too slowly to external change, even though it provides security, stability and continuity (Leavitt 2003). Victor and Stephens (1994), however, argue that bureaucracy is the appropriate organisational form for post-enlightenment thought and for society undergoing industrialisation, and that it furthermore had its consequences for a society that had been previously based upon simple handicraft production. In other words, it is not the case that older, bureaucratic organisational forms had developed in some organic, consequence-free way and that more recent forms did not; rather, it is claimed, both had a profound impact upon society. This does not necessarily imply that organisational change is driven by technological change, but that other factors such as growing pressure upon investment and other resources drives change in both the business and welfare sectors. It should also be acknowledged in passing that bureaucracy can be seen as 'rationalised patriarchy', within which the practice of male homosociability positions women in subordinate roles (Savage and Witz, 1992; Wilson, 1996); we will return to the issue of gender in relation to change in social work below.

Organisational change in social work

Coulshed et al (2006), in the course of several editions of their book on management in social services, were able to look at changes in the organisational context of social work in connection with the various management theories that had informed these changes. So, for example, they were able to discuss the culture change in social services brought in by the total quality management philosophy (see **Chapter Nine**).

Although there is a good deal of material on the subject of organisational change in Coulshed et al's (2006) book, their main interest is in how organisation change can be affected by leadership. The front-line social worker probably will not be in a position to effect sweeping change in the organisational culture of a social services area office. Indeed, recent national child protection inquiries appear to have borne out the fact that nothing but major intervention at the most senior level, such as the recent takeover of Doncaster council, stands a realistic chance of changing some aspects of the organisation such as employee working practices. It seems unlikely therefore that team leaders or even middle-level managers can initiate sweeping organisational change in social services although, like social workers, they may well be agents and instruments of change (see **Chapter Ten**).

Politics of organisational change in social work

It could be argued that the influence of policy and politics on social work could effectively reduce a chapter on change in British social work organisations to a history of British social policy over the past century. The work of Parton (1985) and others on the politics and even the social construction of child protection scandals can be seen as supporting this sense that it is a discourse of the powerful which in the end brings about the organisational change and delivery of social work.

This gives us a sense that social work is something of a political football, prey perhaps to the whims of politicians. Challis (1990) has argued that this is not the case, however. She maintains that the waves of organisational change in social work have been to a large extent self-inflicted. This would support the view that social work organisations have their own internal dynamics, which are relatively autonomous of national politics. Although Challis was primarily concerned with the impending changes of the 1990s, she also analysed the structure of social services at that point in terms of the various tensions social services had experienced historically as an organisation.

History of organisational change in social work

Since the creation of local authority social services departments at the beginning of the 1970s a key source of tension has been the melding together of residential services and fieldwork services. This organisational 'given' continues to exercise managers, change agents and staff as they try to create the elusive 'seamless web' of direct work and fieldwork services so often recommended in government-commissioned reports. Another key problem was identified by Timms (1970) on the eve of the creation of local authority social services departments, that of joining generic provision with specialist skills in such a way that the client was not visited endlessly by functionally separate teams of specialists asking the same questions. A third problem has been that of preventing the growing new local authority personal social services departments from becoming the large, impersonal bureaucracies of the Poor Law that they were designed to replace (Townsend, 1962). Community working and 'going local' in the 1980s (see Pierson, 2007) can also be seen as a reorganisation strategy with impacts on the front-line social worker.

The life-stage organisational divisions created in many authorities from the 1980s onwards, that is, the separation of children and families and adult services, can be seen as an organisational change strategy to prevent clients from being passed from one department to another, albeit at the cost of reinforcing divides between these services. Indeed, Massey and Pyper (2005) have argued that, if public service reorganisation under the Conservative government of the 1980s and early 1990s was about value for money, then under the New Labour government in the late 1990s it was about consumer rights and responsiveness to customers, building to an extent upon selected themes of the previous administration.

It is also possible to see the 'hollowing out' of social services organisations, by the removal of a layer of management, as a continuation of attempts to prevent the alienation of clients. The assumption is that flatter, local management leads to a more flexible, consumer-responsive service that is also cheaper to run and has more of its resources spent on front-line services (see also **Chapter Eight**). It should also be noted that different organisational forms have been developed in different authorities (Challis, 1990; Lambley, 2009). Of course, the organisational structures of county and metropolitan authorities were significantly different to begin with, but many of these changed shape during the period of organisational change in the 1990s. Some local authority social services departments did away with their team leaders (unsurprisingly, the lowest level of management was often the one to be shed), an arrangement that could result in less frequent supervision provided by the next layer of management, making this a fraught job indeed, for both supervisee and supervisor. Other authorities merged life stages or geographical areas as ways of losing a tier of management. Challis (1990) has argued that diversity in organisational forms increased year on year in social services after the Local Authority Social Services Act 1970 which established local authority social services departments. Prior to this Children's Departments were of comparatively routine form, and immediately following the Act there were only a small number of permutations of geographical, life–stage and specialism divisions that, together with the fieldwork and residential divide, structured social services departments. The organisational charts from Challis (1990) (Figures 11.2, 11.3 and 11.4) illustrate the consequences for chain of accountability, for the individual social worker, of just geographical, functional, and client group management.

By today's standards the considerable diversity uncovered by Challis in 1990 seems modest. Now the field is even richer: separate directorates for children's and adults' services; children's services run by private educational companies; adults' services with layers of health trust management. How many layers of management the social worker has nowadays depends upon which service she is working for.

Perhaps the important message overall is that social work services can be delivered by a number of different organisational structures. None of these structures entirely resolves the enduring problems of efficient social services delivery, which gives the new manager a perennial pretext for organisational change, even in the absence of new policy initiatives from central government. This is presumably what Challis (1990) means when she says that waves of organisational change in social services have been largely self-inflicted.

Figure 11.2: Three alternative structures of a social services department

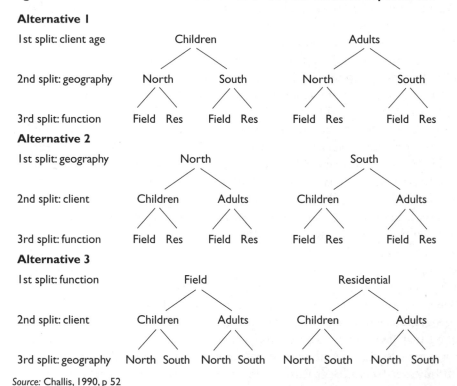

Alternative 1

1st split: client age	Children				Adults			
2nd split: geography	North		South		North		South	
3rd split: function	Field	Res	Field	Res	Field	Res	Field	Res

Alternative 2

1st split: geography	North				South			
2nd split: client	Children		Adults		Children		Adults	
3rd split: function	Field	Res	Field	Res	Field	Res	Field	Res

Alternative 3

1st split: function	Field				Residential			
2nd split: client	Children		Adults		Children		Adults	
3rd split: geography	North	South	North	South	North	South	North	South

Source: Challis, 1990, p 52

Figure 11.3: Management structure in a geographically split social services department

1st split: geography
2nd split: geographic
3rd split: geographic or functional or client group
4th split: geographic or functional or client group

The line management structure within this SSD for a basic social worker is:

Social worker

↓

Senior social worker

↓

District manager

↓

Divisional manager

↓

Director

Source: Challis, 1990, p 26

Figure 11.4: Management structure in a geographically then client-based split social services department

1st split: geography
2nd split: geographic
3rd split: client group
4th split: functional

The line management structure for a basic grade social worker within this SSD is:

Social worker

↓

Senior social worker

↓

Team leader

↓

Districy manager

↓

Assistant director

↓

Deputy director

↓

Director

Source: Challis, 1990, p 29

Business process re-engineering

Buchanan (2003) noted the increasing frequency of restructuring over the past 15 years, from five years to three years to every 15 months. He described the results of this as mixed and the process as sometimes bad for staff morale and retention.

The Department of Health's Quality Protects programme, launched in 1998 to support local authorities in improving their services to children, could be considered one of these restructuring initiatives. It is also possible to understand Quality Protects as a version of the total quality management initiative of the 1980s (see **Chapter Nine**). Buchanan also studied the application of business process re-engineering (BPR) to the operating theatres at Leicester Hospital in 1997. Obolensky (1994) described BPR as an alternative to total quality management and 'continuous improvement' programmes of change and as a model that also rejects organisational culture change approaches as being simply too slow (they are seen to take at least five years to produce significant organisational change). Instead, BPR tracks client trails, reassigning or re-engineering teams, services and tasks to expedite or improve outcomes. An example of this could be physically relocating services and service teams to enable easier client access. In a tellingly titled article, 'Reengineering work: don't automate, obliterate', Hammer (1990) returned, as others had, to the consideration of Japanese competition and the Ford Motor Company in the 1980s (see **Chapter One**). An information technology consultant, Hammer noted that IT was being used in the 1980s by many companies to 'pave cowpaths', as he put it, leaving organisational structures unchanged. Hammer proposed instead that, like Ford, corporations should use IT to reorganise structure as well, instead of, for example, simply using PCs to do bureaucratic paperwork, which, he argued, does not actually produce a better product or a more satisfied customer (Hammer, 1990). Putting IT terminals in council offices for customers to use is therefore perhaps an example of BPR.

Buchanan's 1997 study found that, in practice, the political agendas of occupational groups impeded the implementation of BPR. Some staff wanted to focus on re-engineering the operating theatres, others the entire client trail.

In criticism, Grint (1994) contends that the rise of BPR in the early 1990s had less to do with the internal coherence or rationality of the BPR idea and much more to do with its coincidence with the *zeitgeist* and public opinion and its novelty and contrast to the previous culture. Another criticism of BPR is that it is behavioural in its focus, and ignores contextual factors such as work group history and status differences between staff professional groupings.

Understanding change in social work

What do we understand about the direction of change in social work organisations? If we know where we have come from, do we also know where we are heading? Farrell and Morris (2003) argue that social work organisations (along with other public sector organisations) are not in fact heading in the direction of a 'post-bureaucratic' state. They contend that a centralised bureaucracy now administers a marketised public sector, which they call a 'neo-bureaucratic' form of organisation. They argue that these changes are irreversible. However, the social workers they interviewed saw the persistence of a public service and care ethic in the new organisations and management, suggesting strong continuities from

the 'bureaucratic' past. Social work careers today increasingly resemble Kanter's (1994) post-corpocratic careers, as temporary and part-time employment through agencies replaces the one-authority career, and professional ethics and values replace organisational loyalty.

Another theme in recent social services organisational change has been the residualisation of local authority provision, understood as a closer focus upon their 'default' role. This can be seen as a reversion to their 'core business' (Hammer, 1990).

In an attempt to understand recent public sector change Grungalis et al (2003) looked at changes in the organisational structure of housing benefit workers. The changes included a move to the contracting-in of agency workers in significant numbers to fill vacant posts. Grungalis et al found that where this happened one side-effect was the constraining of the worker's discretion because work that was outsourced was managed differently from that undertaken by 'in-house' staff, with closer managerial monitoring replacing or reducing employees' discretion. Partly this was because agency staff were thought to have fewer skills and were consequently given access to a narrower range of skill work than their conventionally employed counterparts. Meanwhile staff employed on permanent contracts were given and exercised greater amounts of responsibility, with positive results for both their skills and for the work processed. Although social work is not the same as housing benefit work, the growing tendency towards the employment of agency social workers to fill vacancies could also be argued to constrain the decision-making process in social work.

However, Postle and Gorman (2003) argue that the application of management theories of organisation to welfare organisations has beneficially moved service user consultation into the frame and, if anything, managers are under-trained rather than over-trained (Kakabadse et al, 2005).

Gender

Given the gendered nature of social work organisations we must ask, as we have done in other chapters, what is the impact of gender on experiencing organisational change. Newman and Mooney (2004) and also Robbins (2003) discuss the intensive and perceived unskilled character of much work in welfare organisations. They argue that there is a dual labour market in social care organisations, which means that some employees are in stronger full-time and permanent positions, while others are in part-time and temporary work and these will mostly be women on the front line of social care services. Organisational change tends to have its most sweeping consequences at the sharp end of services and so disproportionately affects female staff and also their often female service users.

Conclusion

It has been claimed that the banking crisis of 2008 has taught us that some aspects of organisations are very resistant to change. Despite media calls for an end to the 'bonus culture' of banks (which was judged by some to have been a causal factor in the short-termism and poor risk-taking of some banks), substantial bonuses have continued to be paid to senior staff.

If one lesson could be learned from the increasing plurality of organisational forms in which social work is conducted, it is perhaps that the 'street-level bureaucracy' (Lipsky, 1980) immediately surrounding the social worker is the area of the organisation that she most needs to understand, analyse and learn how to work. The composite organisational settings in which many social workers now operate are so complex, extensive and dense, that the dynamics of the immediate organisation are, for most practical purposes, the ones that matter. In short, the influence of the alleged organisation-wide resistance to change in social work may be less important than the dynamics of the social worker's immediate organisational context.

We can usually see organisational change strategies before they are officially implemented, but the context of team, service users and supervision is the one in which 'culture change' and 'tipping point' will actually be meaningful. The focus upon change to self-managing, permeable, networking teams in recent years (Payne, 2000; Grey, 2007; Hughes and Waring, 2007) appears to be in constant conflict with the need to maintain tight financial controls, producing recurrent pressure to revert to the classical 'mechanical bureaucracy'. Social work organisational forms therefore seem to slot-rattle between the two, or perhaps more accurately to settle in a midway position. This may go some way to explaining the apparent resistance to change and also why full service user engagement sometimes seems so elusive.

▶KEY LEARNING POINTS

- Organisational change can have a number of internal and external drivers
- The organisational behaviour literature tends to overemphasise individual responses to change, which have limited predictability
- There are models which offer approaches for managing organisational change, some of which may be familiar to social workers
- Change in welfare organisations tends to follow a cycle, being influenced by local and national political processes
- Welfare organisations can oscillate between front-line empowerment strategies and tight budgetary control

▶SEMINAR ORIENTATION: HOW FAR CAN SOCIAL WORK BE CONSIDERED A NEGOTIATED PROCESS WITH THE CONSUMER?

Reading:

For: Powell, J. (1999) 'Contract management and community care', *British Journal of Social Work*, vol 29, pp 861-75.

Against. Jordan, B. (2001) 'Tough love: social work, social exclusion and the third way' *British Journal of Social Work*, vol 31, pp 527-46.

See also the article: Jones, C. (2001) 'Voices from the front line: state social workers and New Labour', *British Journal of Social Work*, vol 31, pp 547-62.

CHAPTER TWELVE

Conclusion: social workers in organisations

Introduction

In March 2010 the government published an interdepartmental implementation plan *Building a safe and confident future* (HM Government, 2010a) based on the recommendations of the Social Work Task Force in their report on many aspects of social work in England (Burnham and Balls, 2009). In this concluding chapter, we ask what organisational changes might benefit services and to what extent the implementation plan indicates a pathway to such changes.

Organisational impact of the social work plan

According to the 2009 report (Burnham and Balls, 2009), the key organisational expectation of social work employers is that they provide support for social workers to do their jobs effectively. This requirement clearly has implications for teams, management and communication in social work organisations. In particular, *Building a safe and confident future* (HM Government, 2010) highlights supervision (including management and decision making); professional development (implying a culture change in some social work organisations), training and support for frontline managers (involving attention to management style, as well as organisational culture), and a national career structure (requiring social work organisations to look closely at motivation in social work).

As can be seen, these requirements affect the core organisational behaviour areas covered in this book. Potential criticisms of the plan can also be linked to these areas. First, the plan appears to focus, in a rather bureaucratic manner, on predicting social worker demand and on controlling the supply of qualified workers. There is, however, relatively little sense of the market fluctuations reflecting the twitching of government social policy or the changing conditions of service. As we saw in **Chapter Eleven**, one of the criticisms of bureaucracies is that, despite the best intentions, they can be unresponsive, precisely because they operate in this smooth, predicted-certainties manner. **Chapter Eleven** indicated some of the drivers for moving away from bureaucracy, although a tendency towards hyper-bureaucracy was seen to emerge even in competitive tendering and Best Value settings.

Addressing the perceived current state of provision in higher education training of social workers, and in local authority interpretation of standards, the plan appears to suggest a somewhat bureaucratic approach to controlling everything, even down to the interpretation of standards. Some commentators consider this to be almost impossible (for example, Lipsky, 1980). The government wants employers, including local authority social services departments, to cooperate with one another, yet this may run up against political divisions in some areas of the country. Similarly with higher education institutions, which currently compete with one another, especially in a period of shrinking resources. Furthermore, local authorities and local higher education institutions will be forced into working together, which has some potentially positive outcomes, but there is a danger that important organisational differences may be overlooked.

Colleagues at management level in local authority social services settings may also feel that changing the organisational imperatives to supervision may simply shift attention away from some other important aspect of practice. Colleagues also observe that cash-strapped local authorities cannot afford the proposed training of front-line managers, or even for the post-qualifying programme (see GSCC, 2005). The government did commit £200 million funding to this early in 2010, but it remains to be seen what impact that funding will have.

It also remains to be seen how local authorities or the current administration will respond to the first child protection tragedies of the new organisational setup. As Simon (2008) noted in relation to the impact of a murdered child upon a local authority police department: 'a red-ball case puts everybody from the front line to the mayor on 24-hour report' (Simon, 2008, p 21).

External influences on social work organisations

It is interesting to note the general character of recent social policy measures for improving the organisational setting of social work and social work training, so as to enhance the delivery and responsiveness of services. From an organisational point of view, the policy involves closer regulation and national standardisation, measures to improve the inter-organisational communication of large bureaucracies (for example between local authorities and higher education institutions), and better supervisory support for social workers within large bureaucracies. By contrast, current and emerging social policy envisages some very different organisational futures. A larger number of more diverse and smaller social service provider organisations are envisaged, with social entrepreneurs and voluntary sector organisations playing a larger role. The benefits of this are expected to be greater flexibility in response to customer need, as well as more efficient services. The echoes of Japanisation (see **Chapter Six**) are visible in this, as are more recent developments in organisational thinking. However, the responses to recent organisational crises in the world at large (such as the banking crisis), suggest that breaking up large organisations will not be easy. There is also a fear that closer regulation may make organisations ever less flexible. Even so, some permutation of these two strategies seems likely in social services in the foreseeable future.

The organisational challenges confronting the public sector bear more than a passing resemblance to those identified by Kakabadse et al (2004) for large organisations in the private sector. The impact of globalisation upon social services may be mediated via the economy as a whole, as may the impact of internet markets, but the challenge of constructing flexible, demand-responsive service units, permeated by an applied ethical code and drawing on employee and customer diversity, appears to be common to organisations in all sectors.

Grey (2007) has identified the current phase of organisational development as that of 'fast capitalism'. He sees the characteristic organisation of this phase as possessing a culture of continuous organisational change, self management and speeding up; and its managers as change leaders, rather than managers. Similarly, it is possible to see the move to identifying a newly qualified social worker status as involving more change leadership for managers in social work organisations (see **Chapter Eleven**).

Employment and training

Taking the long view, it is possible to see in public service organisations a change from the passive posting of employees to the head-hunting of social workers (there is currently a UK scheme to draw high-fliers from other professions and fast-track them into social work), and a change from the use of civil service commissions and 'trawls' to decentralised decision making at the 'sharp end' of organisations. Social workers are also increasingly employed from agencies on an ad hoc basis (Berman et al, 2001). Such semi-self-employed status can also be seen to square with the recommendations of the social care White Paper, *Building the national care service* (HM Government, 2010b) that the General Social Care Council (GSCC) should focus solely on social work regulation and education and become a body funded by its members.

Organisational changes to social work training and regulation have accelerated in pace over recent years: from the Central Council for Education and Training in Social Work (CCETSW), replaced by the GSCC and other UK nations' care councils in 2001, to the dissolution of the GSCC in England from the summer of 2012, with functions being transferred to the Health Professions Council (which will become the Health and Care Professions Council) (McGregor, 2010; Carson, 2011; Department of Health, 2011). The College of Social Work, substantially modelled on the Royal College of Nursing, has been the subject of political wrangling and seems set to separate some parts of the organisational role of advocacy from social work, as well as that of training quality assurance.

Recommendation 8 of the Social Work Task Force's report (Burnham and Balls, 2009) referred to the creation of dedicated programmes of training and support for front-line social work managers. The suggested 'starting point' for the content of this training is that recommended for managers in adult social care in 2007. These recommendations appear to be fairly traditional management skills such as leadership, budget management, communication, personal skills, understanding organisational culture, and so on, although they are worded in a very abstract way.

They would not be incompatible with almost any of the 'managerial revolution' handbooks of the past thirty years.

Sustainability in social work

A final remark should perhaps be made about the position on organisational change in social work organisations adopted in this book. Hughes and Waring (2007) have suggested that sustainability should be a key consideration in social work service provision. There is a well-established argument for this: not least that sustainable lifestyles and their place within low growth, low consumption economies are increasingly endorsed within an era of restricted resources (Simon-Brown, 2000). There have consequently been initiatives to embed sustainability issues in various university disciplines, including social work (Wilkinson and Bissell, 2005), with local authorities and universities perceived as potential change leaders on the road to sustainable communities (Buchan et al, 2007). Yet, there is a corollary of the argument for ecological good practice that is, if anything, even more relevant to social work: social justice. If people have little investment in the society in which they live, it is futile to try to impress upon them the importance of sustainable lifestyles, conservation or other 'green' practices. The point is therefore that social inclusion, participation and empowerment are not only social work values but also the precondition for the move towards sustainability. From an English perspective at least, the goal of social inclusion and participation is still a much needed part of the social work role. At a time of stringent scrutiny of social services and welfare budgets, social exclusion seems unlikely to diminish in importance. Preliminary reports of these current changes suggest de-layering (for example the merging of organisations or departments and the removal of tiers of management; see **Chapter Eight**), and the reversion to the 'core business' of statutory duties at the cost of preventive work.

A glimmer of light in this rather gloomy prospective future is the inclination of some local authorities to approach the current cycle of belt-tightening as an opportunity to maximise community empowerment through self-management of the limited services and resources available, reflecting to some extent the political agenda of the current Coalition government (Liddle, 2011). Much depends upon how the agenda of organisational change in social services, from providers of services to enablers of community self-government, is implemented. All aspects of organisational behaviour referred to in this book are likely to be involved in such changes and social workers will be called upon to take their part in the reconstruction of welfare organisations. It is hoped that this book proves useful in facing these changes.

▶**KEY LEARNING POINTS**

- The regulatory bodies of social work are currently undergoing organisational change and this is another way in which organisational change has an impact on social workers and social work practice
- The attainment of legal title means that the regulatory body effectively has a default role in specifying the organisational context of social work
- Empowerment and social justice may come into conflict with sustainability issues but are a prerequisite for sustainable practice

Bibliography

Abrahamson, E. (2000) 'Change without pain', *Harvard Business Review*, vol 78, no 4, pp 75-9.

Adair, J. (1986) *Effective teambuilding*, London: Pan Books.

Alvesson, M. and Willmott, H. (2004) 'Identity regulation as organisational control producing the appropriate individual', in M. Hatch and M. Schultz (eds) *Organisational identity: A reader*, Oxford: Oxford University Press, pp 436-65.

Andrew, T. (1999) 'Employment history of social services staff', in S. Balloch, J. McLean and M. Fisher (eds) (1999) *Social services: Working under pressure*, Bristol: The Policy Press, pp 23-42.

Argyris, C. and Schön, D.A. (1974) *Organizational learning: A theory of action perspective*, Reading, MA: Addison-Wesley.

Argyris, C. and Schön, D.A. (1978) *Theory in practice: Increasing professional effectiveness*, San Francisco, CA: Jossey-Bass.

Aronson, J. (1992) 'Women's sense of responsibility for the care of old people', *Gender & Society*, vol 6, no 1, pp 8-29.

Bales, R.F (1950) *Interaction process analysis: A method for the study of small groups*, Boston, MA: Addison-Wesley.

Balloch, S., McLean, J. and Fisher, M. (eds) (1999) *Social services: Working under pressure*, Bristol: The Policy Press.

Barnard, C. (1948) *Organisation and management*, Cambridge, MA: Harvard University Press.

Baron, L. and Straus, M. (1987) 'Four theories of rape: a macrosociological analysis', *Social Problems*, vol 34, no 5, pp 467-88.

Bartunek, J., Walsh, K. and Lacey, C. (2000) 'Dynamics and dilemmas of women leading women', *Organisation Science*, vol 11, no 6, pp 589-610.

Bechky, B. (2006) 'Gaffers, gofers, and grips: role-based co-ordination in temporary organisations', *Organisation Science*, vol 17, no 1, pp 3-21.

Belbin, M. (1981) *Management teams: Why they succeed or fail*, Oxford: Butterworth-Heinemann.

Belbin, R.M. (1993) *Team roles at work*, Oxford: Heinemann.

Belbin, R.M. (1996) *The coming shape of organisations*, Oxford: Heinemann.

Benne, K. and Sheats, P. (1948) 'Functional roles of group members', *Journal of Social Issues*, vol 4, pp 41-9.

Beresford, P. (1980) 'Public participation and the redefinition of social policy', in C. Jones and J. Stevenson (eds) *Yearbook of social policy in Britain 1980–1981*, pp 221-32.

Beresford, P. and Croft, S. (1990) *From paternalism to participation: Involving people in social services*, York: Joseph Rowntree Foundation.

Berger, P. and Luckmann, T. (1967) *The social construction of reality: A treatise in the sociology of knowledge*, London: Allen Lane/Penguin Books.

Berman, E., Bowman, J., West, J. and Van Wart, M. (2001) *Human resource management in public service: Paradoxes, processes, and problems*, London. Sage Publications.

Berne, E. (1963) *The structures and dynamics of organizations and groups*, London: Pitman Medical.

Berridge, D. (1985) *Children's homes*, London: Blackwell.

Bezrukova, K., Jehn, K., Zanutto, S., Sherry, M. and Thatcher, B. (2009) 'Do workgroup faultlines help or hurt? A moderated model of faultlines, team identification, and group performance', *Organisation Science*, vol 20, no 1, pp 35-50.

Biestek, F. (1961) *The casework relationship*, London: Allen & Unwin.

Bissell, G. and Sullivan, P. (2012) 'Failure, communities of practice and the value base of social work', *Critical Social Work*, vol 13, no 1, pp 83-94.

Blake, R. and Mouton, J. (1964) *The managerial grid: Key orientations for achieving production through people*, Houston, TX: Gulf Publishing Company.

Booher, D. (1994) *Communicate with confidence!*, New York, NY: McGraw-Hill Inc.

Booker, C. (1970) *The neophiliacs: A study of the revolution in English life in the 50s and 60s*, London: Fontana.

Boss, M. (1970) *Existential foundations of medicine and psychology*, New York, NY: Jason Aronson.

Bowden, P. (1997) *Caring: Gender-sensitive ethics*, London: Routledge.

Bower, M. (ed) (2005) *Psychoanalytic theory for social work*, London: Practice.

Braverman, H. (1974) *Labour and monopoly capital: The degradation of work in the twentieth century*, New York, NY: Monthly Review Press.

Briggs, T. (1980) 'Obstacles to implementing the team approach in social services agencies', in S. Lonsdale, A. Webb and T. Briggs (eds), *Teamwork in the personal and social services and healthcare: British and American perspectives*, London, Croom Helm, pp 75-89.

Briscoe, F. (2007) 'From iron cage to iron shield? How bureaucracy enables temporal flexibility for professional service workers', *Organisation Science*, vol 18, no 2, pp 297-314.

Brown, A. (1998) *Organisational culture*, 2nd edition, London: Financial Times Management

Brown, A. and Bourne, I. (1996) *The social work supervisor*, Buckingham: Open University Press.

Brown, J. (1980) 'Child abuse: an existential process', *Clinical Journal of Social Work*, vol 8, no 2, pp 108-15.

Brown, J. and Duguid, P. (1991) 'Organisational learning and communities-of-practice: toward a unified view of working, learning, and innovation', *Organisation Science*, vol 2, no 1, pp 40-57.

Brown-Graham, A. and Morgan, J. (2007) 'Community development and affordable housing', in C. Stenberg and S. Austin (eds) *Managing local government services*, Washington, DC: ICMA Press, pp 181-200.

Buchan, G., Spellerberg, I. and Blum, W. (2007) 'Education for sustainability', *International Journal of Sustainability in Higher Education*, vol 8, no 1, pp 4-15.

Buchanan, D.A. (2003) 'The limitations and opportunities of business process engineering in a politicized organizational, climate', *Human Relations*, vol 50, no 1, pp 51-72.

Buchanan, D.A. (2003) 'Demands, instabilities, manipulations, careers: the lived experience of driving change', *Human Relations*, vol 56, no 6, pp 663-74.

Buchanan, D.A. and Huczynski, A. (2004) *Organisational behaviour: An introductory text*, 5th edn, London: Prentice Hall.

Burke, W. (2002) *Organisational change: Theory and practice*, Thousand Oaks, CA: Sage Publishing.

Burnham, A. and Balls, E. (2009) *Building a safe, confident future: The final report of the Social Work Task Force*, London: Department for Children, Schools and Families.

Burnham, J. (1942) *The managerial revolution: Or, what is happening in the world now*, London: Putnam.

Butler, I. and Drakeford, M. (2005) 'Trusting in social work', *British Journal of Social Work*, vol 35, pp 639-53.

Butler, J. (1990) *Gender trouble: Feminism and the subversion of identity*, London: Routledge.

Caplow, T. (1946-7) 'Rumors in war', *Social Forces*, vol 25, pp 298-302.

Carson, D. and Bain, A. (2008) *Professional risk and working with people: Decision making in health, social care and criminal justice*, London: Jessica Kingsley.

Carson, G. (2011) 'Social care workforce regulation in the UK explained', *Community Care*, 16 March.

Caruso, D.R. and Salovey, P. (2004) *The emotionally intelligent manager: How to develop and use the four key emotional skills of leadership*, San Francisco, CA: Jossey-Bass.

Challis, L. (1990) *Organizing public social services*, Aldershot: Ashgate.

Chapman, R. and Greenaway, J. (1980) *The dynamics of administrative reform*, London: Croom Helm.

Charities Aid Foundation (ed) (1993) *Researching the voluntary sector*, West Malling: Charities Aid Foundation.

Clarke, J., Gewirtz, S. and and McLaughlin, E. (eds) (2000) *New managerialism, new welfare?*, London: Sage Publications.

Coates, J. (2009) *Women talk: Conversations between women friends*, Oxford: Blackwell.

Cockburn, J. (1990) *Team leaders and team managers in social services*, Norwich: University of East Anglia.

Cocteau, J. (1937) *Opium: The diary of a cure*, London: Peter Owen.

Collins, D. (2000) *Management fads and buzzwords: Critical-practical perspectives*, London: Routledge.

Coulshed, V. (1991) *Social work practice: An introduction*, London: Macmillan Education.

Coulshed, V., Mullender, A., Jones, D. and Thompson, N. (2006) *Management in social work*, third edn, Basingstoke: Palgrave Macmillan.

Cousins, C. (2010) '"Treat me don't beat me"… exploring supervisory games and their effect on poor performance management', *Practice*, vol 22, no 5, pp 281-92.

Cowling, A.G. and Stanworth, M.J. (1977) *Behavioural sciences for managers*, London: Arnold.

Dahl, R. (1963) *Modern political analysis*, Englewood Cliffs, NJ: Prentice-Hall.

Davis, K.E. (1953) 'Management communication and the grapevine', *Harvard Business Review*, vol 31, pp 43-9.

Davis, T. (1985) 'Managing culture at the bottom', in R. Kilmann, M. Saxton and R. Serpa (eds) *Gaining control of the corporate culture*, San Francisco, CA: Jossey Bass, pp 163-83.

Dawson, S. (1996) *Analyzing organisations*, 3rd edn, London: Macmillan.

Deal, T. and Kennedy, A. (1982) *Corporate cultures: The rites and rituals of corporate life*, London: Addison-Wesley.

Deal, T. and Kennedy, A. (1999) *The new corporate cultures*, London: Texere.

Department of Health (2011) *Enabling excellence*, White Paper, Norwich: The Stationery Office.

Ditton, J. (1977) *Part-time culture: An ethnography of fiddling and pilferidge*, London: Macmillan.

Dominelli, L. (2002) *Anti-oppressive social work theory and practice*, Basingstoke. Palgrave Macmillan.

Dressel, P. (1987) 'Patriarchy and social welfare work', *Social Problems*, vol 34, no 3, June, pp 294-309.

Drucker, P.F. (1955) *The practice of management*, Oxford: Heinemann.

Drucker, P.F. (1959) *Landmarks of tomorrow: A roadmap to the next period in history*, London: Heinemann.

Drucker, P.F. (1969) *The age of discontinuity: Guidelines to our changing society*, New York, NY: Harper & Row

Drucker, P.F. (1974) *Management: Tasks, responsibilities, practices*, London: Butterworth-Heinneman.

Drucker, P.F. (1989) *The new realities: In government and politics, in economics and business, in society and world view*, London: Mandarin.

Durkheim, E. (1964) *The division of labour in society*, trans. G. Simpson, New York, NY: The Free Press.

Dustin, D. (2007) *The McDonaldization of social work*, Farnham: Ashgate.

Engelbrecht, L. (2010) 'A strengths perspective on supervision of social workers: an alternative management paradigm within a social development context', *Social Work and Social Sciences Review*, vol 14, no 1, pp 47-58.

Erikson, E. (1980) *Identity and the life cycle*, London: W.W. Norton.

Erikson, E. (1994) *Identity: Youth and crisis*, London: W.W. Norton.

Etzioni, A. (ed) (1969) *The semi-professions and their organisation*, New York, NY: Free Press.

Farrell, C. and Morris, J. (2003) 'The "neo-bureaucratic" state: professionals, managers and professional managers in schools, general practices and social work', *Organization*, vol 10, no 1, pp 129-56.

Fast, J. (1970) *Body language*, New York, NY: M. Evans & Co.

Fayol, H. (1949) *General and industrial management*, trans. Constance Storrs, London: Sir Isaac Pitman & Sons.

Festinger, L. (1962) *A theory of cognitive dissonance*, London: Tavistock.

Fleishman, E. and Harris, E. (1962) 'Patterns of leadership behaviour related to employee grievances and turnover', *Personnel Psychology*, vol 15, pp 43-56.

Fligstein, N. (1992) 'The social construction of efficiency', in M. Zey (ed) *Decision making: Alternatives to rational choice models,* London: Sage Publications, pp 351-76.

Ford, H. (1922) *My life and work*, Garden City, NY: Garden City Publishing.

Foucault, M. (1975) *Discipline and punish: The birth of the prison*, London: Allen Lane.

Frantzve, J.L. (1983) *Behaving in organizations: Cases and exercises*, Upper Saddle River, NJ: Prentice Hall.

French, J.R.P. and Raven, B. (1959) 'The bases of social power', in D. Cartwright (ed) *Studies in social power*, Ann Arbor, MI: University of Michigan Press.

Furness, S. and Gilligan, P. (2006) 'The role of religion and spirituality in social work practice: views and experiences of social workers and students', *British Journal of Social Work*, vol 36, no 4, pp 617-37.

Furness, S. and Gilligan, P. (2010) *Religion, belief and social work: Making a difference*, Bristol: The Policy Press.

Galambos, L. (1970) 'The emerging organisational synthesis in modern American history', *Business History Review,* vol 44, pp 279-90.

Galbraith, J. (1958) *The affluent society*, London: Hamish Hamilton.

Gallie, D. (1991) 'Patterns of skill change: upskilling, deskilling, or the polarisation of skills?', *Work, Employment & Society*, vol 5, no 3, pp 319-51.

Galloway, G., Wilkinson, P. and Bissell, G. (2008) 'Empty space or sacred place? Place and belief in social work training', *Journal of Practice Teaching and Learning*, vol 8, no 3, pp 28-47.

George, D. (1971) 'Social work in the army', in R. Little (ed) *Handbook of military institutions*, Beverly Hills, CA: Sage Publications.

Gibelman, M. and Furman, R. (2008) *Navigating human service organisations*, Chicago, IL: Lyceum Books.

Gilbreth, F. (1911) *Motion study: A method for increasing the efficiency of the workman*, New York, NY: Van Nostrand.

Glastonbury, B., Bradley, R. and Orme, J. (1987) *Managing people in the personal social services*, Chichester: John Wiley.

Godkin, A. (1980) 'Identity and place: clinical applications based on notions of rootedness and uprootedness', in A. Buttimer and D. Seamon (eds) *The human experience of place and space*, London: Croom Helm, pp 73-85.

Goffman, E. (1957) 'Alienation from interaction', *Human Relations*, vol 10, no 1, pp 47-60.

Goleman, D. (1995) *Emotional intelligence: How it can matter more than IQ*, London: Bloomsbury.

Goleman, D. (1998) *Working with emotional intelligence*, London: Bloomsbury.

Goleman, D. (2002) *Primal leadership: Realizing the potential of emotional intelligence*, Boston, MA: Harvard Business Press.

Golensky, M. (2011) *Strategic leadership and management in nonprofit organizations*, Chicago, IL: Lyceum Books.

Gongla, P. and Rizzuto, C. (2001) 'Evolving communities of practice: IBM global services experience', *IBM Systems Journal*, vol 40, no 4, pp 842-63.

Gould, N. (1998) *Social work and the learning organisation*, London: Macmillan.

Gould, N. (2000) 'Becoming a learning organisation: a social work example', *Journal of Social Work Education*, vol 19, no 6, pp 585-96.

Gould, N. and Baldwin, M. (eds) (2004) *Social work, critical reflection and the learning organisation*, Aldershot: Ashgate.

Gray, I., Field, R. and Brown, K. (2010) *Effective leadership, management and supervision in health and social care*, Exeter: Learning Matters.

Gray, J. (1992) *Men are from Mars, women are from Venus: A practical guide for improving communication and getting what you want in your relationships*, London: Harper Collins.

Grey, C. (2007) *A very short, fairly interesting and reasonably cheap book about studying organisations*, London: Sage Publications.

Grimwood, C. and Popplestone, R. (1992) *Women, management and care*, Basingstoke: Palgrave Macmillan.

Grint, K. (1994) 'Re-engineering history: social resonances and business process re-engineering', *Organization*, vol 1, no 1, pp 179-201.

Grubner, C. and Stefanov, H. (eds) (2002) *Gender in social work: Promoting equality*, Lyme Regis: Russell House.

Grungalis, I., Vincent, S. and Hebson, G. (2003) 'The future of professional work? The rise of the network form and the decline of discretion', *Human Resource Management Journal*, vol 13, no 2, pp 45-59.

GSCC (2002) *Codes of practice for social care workers and employers*, London: GSCC.

GSCC (2005) *Post-qualifying framework for social work education and training*, London: GSCC.

Hadley, R. and Hatch, S. (1981) *Social welfare and the failure of the state: Centralised social services and participatory alternatives*, London: Allen & Unwin.

Hafford-Letchfield, T. (2008) *Leadership and management in social care*, London: Sage Publications.

Hall, A., Hockey, J. and Robinson, V. (2007) 'Occupational cultures and the embodiment of masculinity: hairdressing, estate agency and firefighting', *Gender, Work & Organisation*, vol 14, no 6, p 534-51.

Hall, T. and Hall, P. (1980) *Part-time social work*, London: Heinemann.

Hamel, G. and Prahalad, C.K. (1994) *Competing for the future: Breakthrough strategies for seizing control of the industry and creating markets of tomorrow*, Boston, MA: Harvard Business Press.

Hammer, M. (1990) 'Reengineering work: don't automate, obliterate', *Harvard Business Review*, Jul/Aug, pp 104-12.

Hammick, M., Freeth, D.S., Goodsman, D. and Copperman, J. (2009) *Being interprofesssional*, Cambridge: Polity.

Handy, C. (1978) *The gods of management*, Harmondsworth: Penguin.

Handy, C. (1993) *Understanding organisations*, London: Penguin.

Harlow, E. (2000) 'New managerialism and social work: changing women's work', in E. Harlow and J. Lawler (eds) *Management, social work and change*, Aldershot: Ashgate, pp 73-92.

Harlow, E. and Webb, S. (eds) (2003) *Information and communication technologies in the welfare services*, London: Jessica Kingsley.

Harris, J. (1998) 'Scientific management, bureau-professionalism, new managerialism: the labour process of state social work', *British Journal of Social Work*, vol 28, pp 839-62.

Harris, J. (2003) *The social work business*, London: Routledge.

Harris, J. and McDonald, C. (2000) 'Post-Fordism, the welfare state and personal social services: a comparison of Australia and Britain', *British Journal of Social Work*, vol 30, pp 51-70.

Harrison, I. (1956) *Agatha Harrison: An impression by her sister Irene Harrison*, London: Allen & Unwin.

Harrison, R. (1972) 'Understanding your organisation's character', *Harvard Business Review*, vol 50, pp 119-28.

Harvey, C. (1980) *Social welfare archives in Britain and the USA*, Museum of Social Work Occasional Papers No 1, Glasgow: Heatherbank Press.

Hatch, M. and Schultz, M. (eds) (2004) *Organisational identity: A reader*, Oxford: Oxford University Press.

Hawkins, P. and Shohet, R. (2000) *Supervision in the helping professions:An individual, group and organisational approach*, 2nd edn, Maidenhead: Open University Press.

Hawkins, P. and Shohet, R. (2006) *Supervision in the helping professions*, 3rd edn, Maidenhead: Open University Press.

Hayden, C., Goddard, J., Gorin, S. and Van Der Spek, N. (1999) *State child care: Looking after children?*, London: Jessica Kingsley.

Hearn, J. and Parkin, P.W. (2001) *Gender, sexuality and violence in organisations*, London: Sage Publications.

Hearn, J., Harlow, E. and Parkin, P.W. (1992) 'Sexuality and social work organisations', in P. Carter, J. Hearn and M.K. Smith (eds) *Changing social work and welfare*, London: Sage Publications, pp 131-43.

Heidegger, M. (1927) *Being and time*, London: Routledge & Kegan Paul.

Henderson, J. and Forbat, L. (2002) 'Relationship-based social policy: personal and political', in J. Henderson and D. Atkinson (eds) *Managing care in context*, London: Routledge.

Herzberg, F., Mausner, B. and Snyderman, B. (1959) *The motivation to work*, 2nd edn, New York, NY: John Wiley.

Herzberg, F. (1968) *Work and the nature of man*, London: Staples Press.

Hewlett, S. (2002) 'Executive women and the myth of having it all', *Harvard Business Review*, vol 80, no 44, April, pp 66-73.

Higham, P. (2009) *Post-qualifying practice*, London: Sage Publications.

HM Government (2010a) *Building a safe and confident future: Implementing the recommendations of the Social Work Task Force*, London: Department for Children, Schools and Families.

HM Government (2010b) *Building the National Care Service*, White Paper, Norwich: The Stationery Office.

Hodgkinson, G. and Sparrow, P. (2002) *The competent organisation*, Buckingham: Open University Press.

Hodgson, D. (2004) 'Project work: the legacy of bureaucratic control in the post-bureaucratic organization', *Organization*, vol 11, no 1, pp 81-100.

Holder, D. and Wardle, M. (1981) *Teamwork and the development of the unitary approach*, London: Routledge & Kegan Paul.

Holt, R. (2004) 'Risk management: the talking cure', *Organization*, vol 11, no 2, pp 251-70.

Horder, W (1999) 'Absent without leave: a gender perspective on the management of staff sickness in social services', *Critical Social Policy*, vol 19, no 2, pp 257-70.

Howe, D. (2008) *The emotionally intelligent social worker*, Basingstoke: Palgrave Macmillan.

Hughes, M. and Waring, M. (2007) *Organisations and management in social work*, London: Sage Publications.

Hughes, R. (1994) *Culture of complaint: A passionate look into the ailing heart of America*, New York, NY: Oxford University Press.

Hugman, R. (1991) *Power in caring professions*, London: Macmillan.

Hyde, P. and Davies, H. (2004) 'Service design, culture and performance: collusion and co-production in health care', *Human Relations*, vol 57, no 11, pp 1407-27.

Iannello, K. (1992) *Decisions without hierarchy: Feminist interventions in organisation theory and practice*, London: Routledge.

Illich, I. (1983) *Gender*, London: Marion Boyars.

Irving, A. and Young, T. (2006) 'Paradigm for pluralism: Mikhail Bakhtin and social work practice', *Social Work*, vol 47, no 1, pp 19-29.

Jackson, N. and Carter, P. (2000) *Rethinking organisational behaviour*, Harlow: Pearson.

James, B. (1985) *Business wargames*, Harmondsworth: Penguin.

Janis, I. (1972) *Victims of groupthink*, Boston, MA: Houghton Mifflin.

Jaspers, K. (1931) *Man in the modern age*, London: RKP.

Jaspers, K. (1932) *Philosophy*, three volume set, London: Routledge & Kegan Paul.

Jelphs, K. and Dickinson, H. (2008) *Working in teams*, Bristol: The Policy Press.

Jenson, J., Laufer, J. and Maruani, M. (eds) (2000) *The gendering of inequalities: Women, men and work*, Aldershot: Ashgate.

Jeong, S.H., Lee, T., Kim, I.S., Lee, M.H. and Kim, M.J. (2007) 'The effect of nurses' use of the principles of learning organisation on organisational effectiveness', *Journal of Advanced Nursing*, vol 58, no 1.

Jermier, J. and Clegg, S. (1994) 'Critical issues in organization science', *Organization Science*, vol 5, no 1, pp 1-13.

Jermier, J., Slocum, J., Fry, L. and Gaines, J. (1991) 'Organizational subcultures in a soft bureaucracy: resistance behind the myth and façade of an official culture', *Organization Science*, vol 2, no 2, pp 170-94.

Jewkes, R. (1998) 'Why do nurses abuse patients? Reflections from South African obstetric services', *Social Science and Medicine*, vol 47, no 11, pp 1781-95.

Johnson, C. (2010) 'A framework for ethical practice of Action Learning', *Action Learning, Research and Practice*, vol 7, no 3, pp 267-83.

Jones, C. (2001) 'Voices from the front line: state social workers and New Labour', *British Journal of Social Work*, vol 31, pp 547-62.

Jones, C. and Munro, R. (eds) (2005) *Contemporary organisation theory*, Oxford: Blackwell.

Jordan, B. (2001) 'Tough love: social work, social exclusion and the Third Way', *British Journal of Social Work*, vol 31, pp 527-46.

Kakabadse, A., Bank, J. and Vinnicombe, S. (2004) *Working in organisations*, second edn, Aldershot: Gower.

Kakabadse, N., Kakabadse, A. and Kouzmin, A. (2005) 'After the re-engineering: rehabilitating the ICT factor in strategic organisational change through outsourcing', *Problems and Perspectives in Management*, no 1, pp 55-71.

Kane, J. (2006) 'School exclusions and masculine, working-class identities', *Gender and Education*, vol 18, no 6, pp 673-85.

Kanter, R. (1977) *Men and women of the corporation*, New York, NY: Basic Books.

Kanter, R. (1985) *The change masters: Innovation and expertise in the American corporation*, London: Jossey-Bass.

Kanter, R. (1994) *When giants learn to dance*, London: Simon & Schuster.

Kennedy, C. (2002) *Guide to the management gurus*, London: Random House Business Books.

Kipnis, D. and Schmidt, S.M. (1980) 'Intra-organizational influence tactics: explorations in getting one's way', *Journal of Applied Psychology*, vol 65, pp 440-52.

Kitchener, M. (2000) 'The "bureaucratization" of professional roles: the case of clinical directors in UK hospitals', *Organization*, vol 7, no 1, pp 129-54.

Koprowska, J. (2005) *Communication and interpersonal skills in social work*, Exeter: Learning Matters.

Korczynski, M. (2003) 'Communities of coping: collective emotional labour in service work', *Organization*, vol 10, no 1, pp 55-79.

Kotter, J. and Schlesinger, L. (1979) 'Choosing strategies for change', *Harvard Business Review*, vol 41, no 2, pp 32-41.

Kubler-Ross, E. (1969) *On death and dying*, Toronto: Macmillan.

Kuhn, T.S. (1970) *The structure of scientific revolutions*, Chicago, IL: Chicago University Press.

Lakoff, R. (2004) *Language and woman's place*, Oxford: Oxford University Press.

Lambley, S. (2009) *Proactive management in social work practice*, Exeter: Learning Matters.

Landry, C. (1985) *What a way to run a railroad: An analysis of radical failure*, London: Comedia.

Lave, J. and Wenger, E. (1991) *Situated learning: Legitimate peripheral participation*, Cambridge: Cambridge University Press.

Lawler, J. and Bilson, A. (2009) *Social work management and leadership: Managing complexity with creativity*, London: Routledge.

Leavitt, H. (2003) 'Why hierarchies thrive', *Harvard Business Review*, March, pp 96-1022.

Lee, J. (2001) *The empowerment approach to social work practice: Building the beloved community*, New York, NY: Columbia University Press.

Lees, R. (1971) 'Social work 1925-1950', *British Journal of Social Work*, vol 4, no 1, pp 371-9.

Lesser, E. and Storck, J. (2001) 'Communities of practice and organisational performance', *IBM Systems Journal*, vol 40, no 4, pp 831-42.

Liddle, R. (2011) 'Inclusive growth: a new European mission for social democracy', in S. Katwaller and E. Stetter (eds) *Europe's Left in the crisis*, London: Fabian Society.

Lipsky, M. (1980) *Street level bureaucrats: Dilemmas of the individual in public services*, New York, NY: Russell Sage Foundation.

Lishman, J. (1994) *Communication in social work*, London: Macmillan.

Loch, C. (1905) *The Elberfeld system*, Occasional Papers of the Charity Organisation Society Third Series, London: COS Publications.

Lombard, D. (2009a) 'New ADCS chief vows to restore morale to children's social work', *Community Care*, 9 April.

Lombard, D. (2009b) 'Support shortfall leaves staff on brink of burnout', *Community Care*, 21 April.

Lukes, S. (1974) *Power: A radical view*, London: Macmillan.

Lupton, B. (2006) 'Explaining men's entry into female-concentrated occupations: masculinity and social class', *Gender, Work and Organization*, vol 13, no 2, pp 103-28.

Lymbery, M. (1998) 'Care management and professional autonomy', *British Journal of Social Work*, vol 28, pp 863-85.

McClelland, D.C. (1965) 'Toward a theory of motive acquisition', *American Psychologist*, vol 20, no 5, pp 321-33.

McClelland, D.C. (1987) *Human motivation*, Cambridge: Cambridge University Press.

McClelland, D.C. and Burnham, D.H. (1976) 'Power is the great motivator', *Harvard Business Review*, vol 73, no 1, pp 126-39.

McClelland, D.C., Atkinson, J., Clark, R. and Lowell, E. (1953) *The achievement motive*, New York, NY: Appleton-Century-Crofts.

McGregor, D. (1960) *The human side of the enterprise*, New York, NY: McGraw Hill.

McGregor, K. (2009) 'One-third of social workers on anti-depressants in South East', *Community Care*, 9 October.

McGregor, K. (2010) 'GSCC functions could shift under White Paper proposals', *Community Care*, 30 March.

McIver, S. (1991) *Obtaining the views of outpatients*, London: King's Fund.

McLean, J. (1999) 'Satisfaction, stress and control over work', in S. Balloch, J. McLean and M. Fisher (eds) *Social services: Working under pressure*, Bristol: The Policy Press, pp 61–85.

McLean, J. (2003) 'Men as a minority: men employed in statutory social care work', *Journal of Social Work*, vol 3, no 1, pp 45–68.

Macpherson, C.B. (1973) *Democratic theory: Essays in retrieval*, Oxford: Oxford University Press.

Maddock, S. (1999) *Challenging women: Gender, culture and organisation*, London: Sage Publications.

Maddock, S. and Parkin, D. (1993) 'Gender culture: women's strategies and choice at work', *Women in Management Review*, vol 8, no 2, pp 3–10.

Mansbach, A. and Bachner, Y. (2009) 'Self-reported likelihood of whistle blowing by social work students', *Social Work Education*, vol 28, no 1, pp 18–29.

Mant, A. (1979) *The rise and fall of the British manager*, revised edn, London: Macmillan.

Manz, C. (1993) *Business without bosses: How self-managing teams are building high-performing companies*, New York, NY: Wiley.

Marshall, P.D. (ed) (2006) *Celebrity culture: A reader*, London: Routledge.

Maslow, A. (1987) *Motivation and personality*, London: Harper and Row.

Massey, A. and Pyper, R. (2005) *Public management and modernisation in Britain*, Basingstoke: Palgrave Macmillan.

Matusov, E., Hayes, R. and Pluta, M.J. (2005) 'Using a discussion web to develop an academic community of learners', *Educational Technology & Society*, vol 8, no 2, pp 16–39.

Mayo, E. (1933) *The human problems of an industrial civilization*, New York, NY: Viking Press.

Merton, R. (1940) 'Bureaucratic structure and personality', *Social Forces*, May, pp 560–80.

Merton, R., Gray, A., Hockey, B. and Selvin, H. (eds) (1952) *Reader in bureaucracy*, Glencoe, IL: The Free Press.

Middleton, L. (1997) *The art of assessment*, Birmingham: Venture Press.

Miech, R. and Elder, G. (1996) 'The service ethic and teaching', *Sociology of Education*, vol 69, July, pp 237–53.

Millward, L., Haslam, A. and Postmes, T. (2007) 'Putting employees in their place: the impact of hot desking on organizational and team identification', *Organization Science*, vol 18, no 4, pp 547–9.

Milner, J. and O'Byrne, P. (1986) 'The impact of failing students on tutors', *Social Work Education*, vol 6, no 1, pp 21–3.

Miner, J., Crane, D. and Vandenberg, R. (1994) 'Congruence and fit in professional role motivation theory', *Organization Science*, vol 5, no 1, pp 86–97.

Mintzberg, H. (1973) *The nature of managerial work*, New York, NY: Harper and Row.

Mintzberg, H. (1979) *The structuring of organizations: A synthesis of the research*, Englewood Cliffs, NJ: Prentice Hall.

Mintzberg, H. (1983) *Power in and around organizations*, Englewood Cliffs, NJ: Prentice Hall.

Mintzberg, H. (2005) *Managers not MBAs: A hard look at the soft practice of managing and management development*, London: Prentice Hall.

Moore, B. (2008) 'Using technology to promote communities of practice (CoP) in social work education', *Social Work Education*, vol 27, no 6, pp 592-600.

Morales, M. (2009) 'Michelle Morales stands up for social work', *Community Care*, 16 October.

Morgan, G. (2006) *Images of organisation*, London: Sage Publications.

Morrison, T. (2001) *Staff supervision in social care: Making a real difference for staff and service users*, Brighton: Pavilion Publishing.

Moss, S.A., Ritossa, D. and Ngu, S. (2006) 'The effect of follower regulatory focus and extraversion on leadership behaviour: the role of emotional intelligence', *Journal of Individual Differences*, vol 27, no 2, pp 93-107.

Mullender, A. and Perrott, S. (1997) 'Social work and organisations', in R. Adams, L. Dominelli and M. Payne (eds) *Social work: Themes, issues and critical debates*, Basingstoke: Palgrave.

Murray, H.A. (ed) (1938) *Explorations in personality: A clinical and experimental study of fifty men of college age*, Harvard, MA: Harvard Psychological Clinic.

Newell, S. (2001) 'Communication' in E. Wilson (ed) *Organisational behaviour reassessed: The impact of gender*, London: Sage Publications, pp 60-85.

Newell, S., Swan, J. and Kautz, K. (2001) 'The role of funding bodies in the creation and diffusion of management fads and fashions', *Organization*, vol 8, no 1, pp 97-120.

Newman, J. and Mooney, G. (2004) 'Doing "Welfare work"', in G. Mooney (ed) *Work: Personal lives and social policy*, Bristol: The Policy Press.

Newman, T. (2003) *Children of disabled parents*, Lyme Regis: Russell House Publishing.

Nixon, D. (2009) '"I can't put a smiley face on": working-class masculinity, emotional labour and service work in the "new economy"', *Gender, Work and Organisation*, vol 16, no 3, pp 300-22.

O'Brien, M. (ed) (1989) *Reproducing the world*, London: Westview Press.

O'Connor, I., Dalgleish, L. and Khan, J. (1984) 'A reflection of the rising spectre of conservatism: motivational accounts of social work students', *British Journal of Social Work*, vol 14, no 1, pp 227-40.

O'Sullivan, T. (1999) *Decision making in social work*, Basingstoke: Palgrave.

O'Sullivan, T. (2010) *Decision making in social work*, 2nd edn, Basingstoke: Palgrave.

Oakland, J. (2000) *Total quality management: Text with cases*, Oxford: Butterworth Heinemann.

Obolensky, N. (1994) *Practical business re-engineering*, London: Kogan Page.

Odiorne, G. (1965) *Management by objectives: A system of managerial leadership*, London: Pitman Publishing.

Opie, A. (2000) *Thinking teams/thinking clients: Knowledge-based teamwork*, New York, NY: Columbia University Press.

Page, M. (1972) *The company savage: Life in the corporate jungle*, London: Coronet Books.

Parsons, T. (1951) *The social system*, New York, NY: The Free Press.

Parsons, T. and Bales, R.F. (1956) *Family: Socialisation and interaction process*, London: Routledge & Kegan Paul.

Parsons, T. and Shils, E. (eds) (1951) *Toward a general theory of action*, Cambridge, MA: Harvard University Press.

Parton, N. (1985) *The politics of child abuse*, Basingstoke: Macmillan.

Pateman, C. (1970) *Participation and democratic theory*, Cambridge: Cambridge University Press.

Payne, M. (1982) *Working in teams*, London: Macmillan.

Payne, M. (2000) *Teamwork in multiprofessional care*, London: Macmillan.

Pearson, G. (1973) 'Social work as the privatised solution of public ills', *British Journal of Social Work*, vol 3, no 2, pp 209-27.

Peci, A. (2009) 'Taylorism in the socialism that really existed', *Organization*, vol 16, no 2, pp 102-17.

Pedler, M., Burgoyne, J. and Boydell, T. (1997) *The learning company: A strategy for sustainable development*, London: McGraw Hill.

Peters, T. (1987) *Thriving on chaos: Handbook for a management revolution*, London: Macmillan.

Peters, T. and Waterman, R. (1982) *In search of excellence*, New York, NY: Harper & Row.

Petrie, S. (2010) 'The commodification of children in need in welfare markets: implications for managers', *Social Work and Social Sciences Review*, vol 14, no 1, pp 9-26.

Pfeffer, J. (1981) *Power in organisations*, London: Harper Collins.

Pheysey, D. (1993) *Organisational cultures*, London: Routledge

Pierson, J. (2007) *Going local: Working in communities and neighbourhoods*, London: Routledge.

Postle, K. (2002) 'Working between the idea and the reality: ambiguities and tensions in care managers' work', *British Journal of Social Work*, vol 32, pp 335-51.

Postle, K. and Gorman, H. (2003) *Transforming community care: A distorted vision?*, Birmingham: Venture Press.

Powell, J. (1999) 'Contract management and community care', *British Journal of Social Work*, vol 29, pp 861-75.

Pratt, M. and Rafaeli, A. (1997) 'Organisational dress as a symbol of multilayered social identities', in M. Hatch and M. Schultz (eds) *Organisational identity: A reader*, Oxford: Oxford University Press, pp 274-311.

Probst, G. and Buchel, B. (1997) *Organisational learning*, London: Prentice Hall.

Raider, M. (1975) 'An evaluation of management by objectives', *Social Casework*, vol 56, no 1, pp 79-83.

Raider, M. (1976) 'A social services model of management by objectives', *Social Casework*, vol 57, no 4, pp 254-64.

Randall, R. and Southgate, J. (1980) *Co-operative and community group dynamics: Or your meetings needn't be so appalling*, London: Barefoot Books.

Ritzer, G. (1993) *The McDonaldization of society*, Thousand Oaks, CA: Pine Forge Press.

Robbins, S. (1993) *Organizational behaviour: Concepts, controversies and applications*, 6th edn, Englewood Cliffs, NJ: Prentice Hall.

Robbins, S. (2003) *Organizational behaviour: Concepts, controversies and applications*, 10th edn, Englewood Cliffs, NJ: Prentice Hall.

Robinson, J. (1972) 'The dual commitment of social workers', *British Journal of Social Work*, vol 2, no 4, pp 471–80.

Rogers, C. (1951) *Client-centred therapy: Its current practice, implications and theory*, New York, NY: Constable Robinson.

Rogoff, B. (1990) *Apprenticeship in thinking: Cognitive development in social context*, New York, NY: Oxford University Press.

Roper, M. (1994) *Masculinity and the British organisation man since 1945*, Oxford: Oxford University Press.

Rylatt, A. (2003) *Winning the knowledge game*, London: Heinemann.

Satyamurti, C. (1983) 'Discomfort and defence in learning to be a helping professional', *Issues in Social Work Education*, vol 3, no 1, pp 27–38.

Savage, C. (1990) *Fifth generation management*, Newton, MA: Butterworth Heinemann.

Savage, C. (1996) *Fifth generation management: Co-creating through virtual enterprising, dynamic teaming, and knowledge networking*, revised edn, Newton, MA: Butterworth Heinemann.

Savage, M. and Witz, A. (eds) (1992) *Gender and bureaucracy*, Oxford: Blackwell.

Schein, E. (1985) *Organisational culture and leadership*, London: Jossey-Bass.

Schlipp, P. (1957) *The philosophy of Karl Jaspers*, New York, NY: Tudor.

Schofield, J. (2001) 'The old ways are the best? The durability and usefulness of bureaucracy in public sector management', *Organization*, vol 8, no 1, pp 77–96.

Schön, D.A. (1973) *Beyond the stable state: Public and private learning in a changing society*, Harmondsworth: Penguin.

Scott, R. (1969) "Professional employees in a bureaucratic structure: social work" in A. Etzioni (ed) *The semi-professions and their organisation*, New York, NY: Free Press, pp 82–140.

Scourfield, J. (2006) 'Gendered organisational culture in child protection social work', *Social Work*, vol 51, no 1, pp 80–2.

Senge, P. (1990) *The fifth discipline*, London: Random House.

Shadwell, A. (1909) *Industrial efficiency: A comparative study of industrial life in England, Germany and America*, London: Longmans Green.

Shamir, B., House, R. and Arthur, M. (1993) 'The motivational effects of charismatic leadership', *Organization Science*, vol 4, no 4, pp 577–94.

Sharland, E. (2006) 'Young people, risk taking and risk making: some thoughts for social work', *British Journal of Social Work*, vol 36, pp 247–65.

Shaw, I. (2004) 'Evaluation for a learning organisation?', in N. Gould and M. Baldwin (eds) *Social work, critical reflection and the learning organisation*, Aldershot: Ashgate, pp 117-28.

Shaw, M.E. (1976) *Group dynamics*, London: McGraw Hill.

Simey, T. (1937) *Principles of social administration*, Oxford: Oxford University Press.

Simon, D. (2008) *Homicide*, New York, NY: Harcourt Brace Jovanovich.

Simon, D. and Burns, E. (1997) *The corner*, New York, NY: Harcourt Brace Jovanovich.

Simon, H. (1945) *Administrative behaviour*, New York, NY: The Free Press.

Simon, H. (1979) *Models of thought*, Vols 1 and 2, Cambridge, MA: MIT Press.

Simon, H., Smithburg, D. and Thompson, V. (1950) *Public administration*, New York, NY: Alfred Knopf.

Simon-Brown, V. (2000) 'Sustainable living: strategies for breaking the cycle of work and spend', *International Journal of Sustainability in Higher Education*, vol 1, no 3, pp 290-6.

Simpson, R. (2005) 'Men in non-traditional occupations: career entry, career orientation and the experience of role-strain', *Gender, Work and Organisation*, vol 12, no 4, pp 363-81.

Simpson, R. and Simpson, I. (1969) 'Women and bureaucracy in the semi professions', in A. Etzioni (ed) *The semi-professions and their organisation*, New York, NY: Free Press, pp 196-265.

Sinsheimer, R. (1969) 'The existential casework relationship', *Social Casework*, vol 50, no 2, pp 67-71.

Skinner, S. (2006) *Strengthening communities: A guide to capacity building for communities and the public sector*, London: Community Development Foundation.

Slater, P. (1995) 'Practice teaching and self-assessment: promoting a culture of accountability in social work', *British Journal of Social Work*, vol 26, pp 195-205.

Smale, G. and Tucson, G. (1988) *Learning for change: Developing staff and practice in social work teams*, London: NISW.

Smith, G. (1969) *Social work and the sociology of organisations*, revised edn, London: Routledge & Kegan Paul.

Smith, M. and Davidson, L. (1991) 'Analyzing jobs: the manager and the job', in M. Smith (ed) *Analysing organisational behaviour*, London: Macmillan.

Smith, R. (2010) 'One in six social workers have more than 40 cases', *Community Care*, 8 September, p 1.

Snow, C.P. (2000) *The masters*, Looe: House of Stratus.

Solas, J. (1994) 'Why enter social work?', *Issues in Social Work Education*, vol 14, no 2, pp 51-63.

Spencer, H. (1874-85) *Principles of sociology, Volumes I–III*, New York, NY: D. Appleton and Company.

Spencer, H. (1884) *The man versus the state*, New York, NY: D. Appleton and Company.

Stamps, D. (1997) 'Communities of practice: learning is social, training is irrelevant?', *Training*, vol 34, no 2, pp 34-43.

Stevens, M. (2008) 'Workload management in social work services: what, why and how?', *Practice*, vol 20, no 4, pp 207-21.

Stevenson, O. (1980) 'Social service teams in the United Kingdom', in S. Lonsdale, A. Webb and T. Briggs (eds) *Teamwork in the personal and social services and healthcare: British and American perspectives*, London: Croom Helm, pp 9-31.

Stoltenberg, D. and Delworth, U. (1987) *Supervising counsellors and therapists*, San Francisco, CA: Jossey-Bass.

Stoner, J.A.F. (1968) 'Risky and cautious shifts in group decisions: the influence of widely held values', *Journal of Experimental Social Psychology*, vol 4, pp 442–459.

Stoner, J.A.F. (1982) *Management*, London: Prentice Hall.

Stouffer, S., Suchman, E., DeVinney, L., Star, S. and Williams Jnr, R. (1949) 'What were the most critical of the army's promotion opportunities?', in R. Merton, A. Gray, B. Hockey and H. Selvin (eds) (1952) *Reader in bureaucracy*, Glencoe, IL: The Free Press, pp 334-9.

Stretch, J. (1967) 'Existentialism: a proposed philosophical orientation for social work', *Social Work*, vol 12, no 4, pp 97-102.

Sutton, H. and Porter, L. (1968) 'A study of the grapevine in a governmental organization', *Personnel Psychology*, vol 21, pp 223-30.

Tannenbaum, A.S. and Schmidt, W.H. (1958) 'How to choose a leadership pattern', *Harvard Business Review*, vol 36, March-April, pp 95-101.

Tanner, D. (1998) 'Empowerment and care management: swimming against the tide', *Health and Social Care in the Community*, vol 6, no 6, pp 447-87.

Taylor, B. (2010) *Professional decision-making in social work practice*, Exeter: Learning Matters.

Taylor, F. (1911) *The principles of scientific management*, London: Harper & Brothers.

Taylor, M. (1994) 'Gender and power in counselling and supervision', *British Journal of Guidance and Counselling*, vol 22, no 3, pp 319-26.

Thompson, N. (1992) *Existentialism and social work*, Aldershot: Avebury.

Thompson, N., Stradling, S., Murphy, M. and O'Neill, P. (1996) 'Stress and organisational culture', *British Journal of Social Work*, vol 26, pp 647-65.

Thyssen, J. (1957) 'The concept of "Foundering" in Jaspers' philosophy', in P. Schlipp (ed) *The philosophy of Karl Jaspers*, New York, NY: Tudor, pp 297-335.

Timms, N. and Mayer, J. (1970) *The client speaks: Working class impressions of casework*, London: Routledge & Kegan Paul.

Tonnies, F. (1955) *Community and Association,* trans. C. Loomis, London: Routledge and Kegan Paul.

Toren, N. (1969) 'Semi-professionalism and social work: a theoretical perspective', in A. Etzioni (ed) *The semi-professions and their organisation*, New York, NY: Free Press, pp 141-95.

Townsend, P. (1962) *The last refuge: A survey of residential institutions for the aged in England and Wales*, London: Routledge and Kegan Paul.

Trice, H. and Beyer, J. (1991) 'Cultural leadership in organizations', *Organization Science,* vol 2, no 2, pp 149-69.

Tsui, M. (2005) *Social work supervision: Contexts and concepts*, London: Sage Publications.

Turner, M. (1984) 'Arriving where we started: learning about failure in social work', *Issues in Social Work Education*, vol 4, no 1, pp 43-54.

Tversky, A. and Kahneman, D. (1981) 'The framing of decisions and the psychology of choice', *Science*, vol 211, no 4481, pp 453-8.

Uttley, S. (1981) 'Why social work? A comparison of British and New Zealand studies', *British Journal of Social Work*, vol 11, no 1, pp 329-40.

Vecchio, R. (2000) *Organizational behaviour: Core concepts*, 4th edn, New York, NY: Dryden Press.

Vecchio, R., Hearn, G. and Southey, G. (1996) *Organisational behaviour*, 2nd edn, Sydney: Harcourt Brace.

Victor, B. and Stephens, C. (1994) 'The dark side of new organizational forms', *Organization Science*, vol 5, no 4, pp 479-82.

Victor, B., Boynton, A. and Stephens-Jahng, T. (2000) 'The effective design of work under total quality management', *Organization Science*, vol 11, no 1, pp 102-17.

Vroom, V. (1964) *Work and motivation*, New York, NY: John Wiley & Sons.

Wageman, R. and Gordon, F. (2005) 'As the twig is bent: how group values shape emergent task interdependence in groups', *Organization Science*, vol 16, no 6, pp 687-700.

Walker, H. (2002) *A genealogy of equality: The curriculum for social work education and training*, London: Woburn Press.

Wasserman, H. (1971) 'The professional social worker in a bureaucracy', *Social Work*, January, pp 89-95.

Watson, T. (1995) *Sociology, work and industry*, third edn, London: Routledge & Kegan Paul.

Watson, T. (2002) *Organising and managing work: Organisational, managerial and strategic behaviour in theory and practice*, Harlow: Pearson.

Webb, B. (1926) *My apprenticeship*, London: Longman.

Weber, M. (1947) *Theory of social and economic organization*, edited by T. Parsons, New York, NY: The Free Press.

Weber, M. (1964) *The theory of social and economic organization*, New York, NY: The Free Press.

Webster, M. (2010) 'Complexity approach to frontline social work management: constructing an emergent team leadership design for a managerialist world', *Social Work and Social Sciences Review*, vol 14, no 1, pp 27-46.

Welshman, J. (1999) 'The social history of social work: the issue of the "problem family", 1940-1970', *British Journal of Social Work*, vol 29, pp 457-76.

Wenger, E. (1998) *Communities of practice: Learning, meaning and identity*, Cambridge: Cambridge University Press.

Wenger, E., McDermott, R. and Snyder, W.M. (2002) *Cultivating communities of practice*, Boston, MA: Harvard Business Press.

West, M. (2004) *Effective teamwork: Practical lessons from organisational research*, second edn, Oxford: Blackwell.

Whyte, W. (1956) *The organisation man*, Harmondsworth: Penguin.

Wiehe, V. (1973) 'Management by objectives in a family service agency', *Social Casework*, March, pp 142-6.

Wiest, B. and Devis, D. (1971) 'Psychiatric and social work services', in R. Little (ed) *Handbook of military institutions*, Beverly Hills, CA: Sage Publications.

Wilensky, H. (1964) 'The professionalisation of everyone?', *American Journal of Sociology*, vol 70, pp 137-58.

Wilkinson, P. and Bissell, G. (2005) 'Social work education and the "place" of placements', *Practice*, vol 17, no 4, pp 285-97.

Wilkinson, P. and Bissell, G. (2007) 'Human geography and questions for social work education', *Journal of Practice Teaching and Learning*, vol 7, no 2, pp 55-68.

Williams, F. (2001) 'In and beyond New Labour: towards a new political ethics of care', *Critical Social Policy*, vol 21, no 4, pp 467-93.

Williams, J. (2000) *Unbending gender: Why family and work conflict and what to do about it*, Oxford: Oxford University Press.

Wilson, E.M. (ed) (2001) *Organisational behaviour reassessed: The impact of gender*, London: Sage Publications.

Wilson, F. (1996) 'Organizational theory: blind and deaf to gender?', *Organization Studies*, vol 17, no 5, pp 825-42.

Wilson, F. (2003) *Organisational behaviour and gender*, Aldershot: Ashgate.

Wilson, F. (2004) *Organisational behaviour and work: A critical introduction*, Oxford: Oxford University Press.

Wilson, H.W. and Hammerton, J.A. (1919) *The Great War: The standard history of the all Europe conflict*, Vol 13, London: Amalgamated Press.

Wittgenstein, L. (1968) *Philosophical investigations.*,3rd edn, Oxford. Blackwell.

Woodroofe, K. (1962) *From charity to social work*, London: Routledge & Kegan Paul.

Wright, P. (1991) 'Motivation in organisations', in M. Smith (ed) *Analyzing organizational behaviour*, London: Macmillan.

Wu, T.-Y. and Hu, C. (2009) 'Abusive supervision and employee emotional exhaustion', *Group and Organization Management*, vol 34, no 2, pp 143-69.

Younghusband, E. (1947) *Report on the employment and training of social workers*, Edinburgh: T&A Constable.

Index